MACMILLAN MODERN NOVELISTS

GRAHAM GREENE

Neil McEwan

MACMILLAN

First published 1988 by
THE MACMILLAN PRESS LTD
Houndmills, Basingstoke, Hampshire RG21 2XS
and London
Companies and representatives
throughout the world

ISBN 0–333–40688–5 (hardcover)
ISBN 0–333–40689–3 (paperback)

A catalogue record for this book is available
from the British Library.

Printed in Hong Kong

Reprinted 1992

Contents

Acknowledgments

I am grateful to Graham Greene and to William Heinemann for permission to quote from: *Stamboul Train, It's a Battlefield, England Made Me, A Gun for Sale, Brighton Rock, The Confidential Agent, The Power and the Glory, The Ministry of Fear, The Heart of the Matter, The End of the Affair, The Quiet American, Loser Takes All, Our Man in Havana, A Burnt-Out Case* and *The Lawless Roads*; to Graham Greene and to The Bodley Head for permission to quote from: *The Comedians, Travels With My Aunt, The Honorary Consul, The Human Factor, Doctor Fischer of Geneva or The Bomb Party, Monsignor Quixote, The Tenth Man, A Sort of Life, Ways of Escape* and *Collected Essays*.

General Editor's Preface

The death of the novel has often been announced, and part of the secret of its obstinate vitality must be its capacity for growth, adaptation, self-renewal and even self-transformation: like some vigorous organism in a speeded-up Darwinian ecosystem, it adapts itself quickly to a changing world. War and revolution, economic crisis and social change, radically new ideologies such as Marxism and Freudianism, have made this century unprecedented in human history in the speed and extent of change, but the novel has shown an extraordinary capacity to find new forms and techniques and to accommodate new ideas and conceptions of human nature and human experience, and even to take up new positions on the nature of fiction itself.

In the generations immediately preceding and following 1914, the novel underwent a radical redefinition of its nature and possibilities. The present series of monographs is devoted to the novelists who created the modern novel and to those who, in their turn, either continued and extended, or reacted against and rejected, the traditions established during that period of intense exploration and experiment. It includes a number of those who lived and wrote in the nineteenth century but whose innovative contribution to the art of fiction makes it impossible to ignore them in any account of the origins of the modern novel; it also includes the so-called 'modernists' and those who in the mid- and late twentieth century have emerged as outstanding practitioners of this genre. The scope is, inevitably, international; not only, in the migratory and exile-haunted world of our century, do writers refuse to heed national frontiers – 'English' literature lays claim to Conrad the Pole, Henry James the American, and Joyce the Irishman – but geniuses such as Flaubert, Dostoevski and Kafka have had an influence on the fiction of many nations.

Each volume in the series is intended to provide an introduction to the fiction of the writer concerned, both for those approaching him or her for the first time and for those who are already familiar with some parts of the achievement in question and now wish to place it in the context of the total *œuvre*. Although essential information relating to the writer's life and times is given, usually in an opening chapter, the approach is primarily critical and the emphasis is not upon 'background' or generalisations but upon close examination of important texts. Where an author is notably prolific, major texts have been selected for detailed attention but an attempt has also been made to convey, more summarily, a sense of the nature and quality of the author's work as a whole. Those who want to read further will find suggestions in the select bibliography included in each volume. Many novelists are, of course, not only novelists but also poets, essayists, biographers, dramatists, travel writers and so forth; many have practised shorter forms of fiction; and many have written letters or kept diaries that constitute a significant part of their literary output. A brief study cannot hope to deal with all these in detail, but where the shorter fiction and the non-fictional writings, public and private, have an important relationship to the novels, some space has been devoted to them.

NORMAN PAGE

Preface

Graham Greene has made more of an impression on the world than any other British novelist writing during the last fifty years. His international reputation owes something to his other gifts, as a traveller, *cinéaste* and journalist who can claim to be at home anywhere and who has succeeded, for more than fifty years, in seeming a distinctly contemporary writer. He appeals, too, as a novelist of ideas, attitudes and commitments, of broad political and religious interest, and as dire and unconsoling as our times deserve. I have tried in my first chapter to show the nature of these allegiances and, in the following chapters, to survey the development of the art which expresses them in novels from the 1930s to the 1980s. Greene is a great story-teller and his stories create a mood and outlook or, in a phrase he has sometimes used and sometimes cavilled at, 'a region of the mind'. He has claimed 'the tragi-comic region of La Mancha' and I have argued that his flair for comedy contributes, however darkly, to the best earlier novels, and that his mature work is most effective in its relations between comic and tragic perceptions of the world.

I have tried to offer readings of the novels which bear in mind, without deference, Greene's points of view, and to show how enjoyable and rewarding they can be for agnostic readers such as myself, as well as for believers of various kinds. Robert Nye once wrote an essay about 'How to read Graham Greene without kneeling'. I have aimed to write in the same spirit.

My father, R. K. McEwan, performed heroically on the Amstrad.

J. N. McE

1

Greene on Greene

If we begin by letting Greene speak for himself, we must contend with his taste for Romantic and paradoxical roles. He offers as 'an epigraph for all the novels' these lines from Browning:

> Our interest's on the dangerous edge of things.
> The honest thief, the tender murderer,
> The superstitious atheist, demi-rep
> That loves and saves her soul in new French books –
> We watch while these in equilibrium keep
> The giddy line midway.[1]

Such giddy characters occur frequently in the novels: the whisky priest who earns martyrdom, Scobie destroyed by pity, and Pyle the innocent destroyer. Paradox is a ruling principle, too, in the public image Greene has created in his two volumes of autobiography, *A Sort of Life* and *Ways of Escape*, in travel books, reviews and essays, and in the novels, especially the late novels *The Honorary Consul* and *Monsignor Quixote*, which allude to their author's various reputations. Any statement he makes or implies about himself or his work is touched by an amused sense that something quite different might equally well be said. He is a natural exile but is at home anywhere; he has a world readership, and is perhaps more admired abroad that at home, but he is very English – '*terriblement anglais*', a French critic is supposed to have said; he belongs to the 'Establishment' but likes underworlds better; driven to succeed, he is half in love with failure; writing has been one of his ways of escape from the pangs of boredom, but he could have been happy in a routine job except for the bedevilling urge to write; he recommends

1

political commitment but is sceptical about politics; Catholicism marks even those novels which do not have Catholic characters or themes, but he is 'not a Catholic writer' – 'detestable term!' and 'the last title to which I had ever aspired'.[2] He likes to be enigmatic, to evade summing-up. 'A reputation,' he says, 'is like a death mask.'[3]

Greene is combative. We may enjoy him as a story teller, an artist in prose, an ironist, a poet of the gracelessness of modern life, an experimenter with characters and ideas; but he insists that his books are weapons directed against targets in the contemporary world which have grown out of his experience as a journalist. Walter Allen has rightly called him a 'romantic anarchist', pointing out at the same time his inclination to authoritarianism, in Catholicism and Communism.[4] Greene belonged to the Communist Party for only four weeks, at the age of nineteen; had he wished to remain, the party would surely have expelled him before long. He has been a Catholic for more than fifty years, but a dissident for most of them. He likes to be troublesome in politics and religion, and he sees it as a writer's duty to cause trouble to anyone in power.[5] In one conflict, with a fascist head of state, he was pleased to find the Church on his side (François Duvalier was excommunicated), but a Church leader who tried to interfere with Greene's writing was scoffed at in an equally famous exchange of views. If we look at Greene on Greene in combat with these two figures, we see characteristics of authority which he finds distasteful. 'Schoolmasterliness' is one way of summarising them. Greene is opposed to almost all the typical beliefs of an Edwardian public schoolmaster: 'England!', Empire, the 'character' that built them, success, persistence in a safe career, respectability and conformity. Belief in God might be thought common ground; but Greene's is not the God of a school chapel. Indifference to – or innocence of – the tragic sense of life is a related feature of those in power which antagonises him, but the complacency of those he derides is connected with a failure in their comic sense, too. A brief survey of Greene's targets provides a sort of introduction to his cast of mind. If he is unsure of his own personality, or wants us to be unsure of it, one clear guide is his hostility to those who are too sure of themselves.

'I don't like Ike,' says the narrator of *The Quiet American* and he speaks for the author. 'I like – well those two – .' The two are Vietnamese peasants baffled by the war in which they are about to be killed (2.2.3). 'I like Ike' was a campaign-button slogan in the time of Eisenhower. Greene has not liked many American presidents, or their supporters, allies, or puppets in the poorer countries. Most infamous among the latter was François 'Papa Doc' Duvalier, President of Haiti, whose reign of terror he portrayed in *The Comedians*. Greene's Introduction to the novel summarises this president's response.

> A liar, a *cretin*, a stool-pigeon . . . unbalanced, sadistic, perverted . . . a perfect ignoramus . . . lying to his heart's content . . . the shame of proud and noble England . . . a spy . . . a drug addict . . . a torturer. (The last epithet has always a little puzzled me.)[6]

This comes from *Graham Greene Demasqué Finally Exposed*, issued by the Haitian Ministry of Foreign Affairs in 1968. Duvalier had earlier criticised the novel in remarks to French newspapermen – *'le livre n'est pas bien écrit . . . le livre n'a aucune valeur'* – which are quoted with pride in the same Introduction. Greene boasts that 'a writer is not so powerless as he usually feels' since 'a pen . . . can draw blood'. It is true that tyrants pay literature the compliment of fearing it, but Greene was, none the less, powerless against Duvalier, who ruled on in Haiti with full American support. The jest about 'the last epithet' is more telling: it sounds civilised in a way Papa Doc would not understand. Referring to Greene's accounts of himself as an opium-smoker, brothel-goer, heavy drinker and 'manic-depressive', it stresses, its quiet tone rightly following the loud fulmination (contrived, as the dots admit), Duvalier's unawareness of how delightedly Greene would smile at the abuse and add it to the legend, or personal myth, he likes to make of his life.

Another case of official disapproval, amusing to Greene, arose in the Catholic Church's 'condemnation' of *The Power and the Glory*. This novel's success in France caused certain French bishops to complain about its unorthodoxy. The condemned author made a good story of what followed.

The methods of censorship are always curiously haphazard. In the 1950s I was summoned by Cardinal Griffin to

Westminster Cathedral and told that my novel *The Power and the Glory*, which had been published ten years before, had been condemned by the Holy Office, and Cardinal Pizzardo required changes which I naturally – though I hope politely – refused to make. Cardinal Griffin remarked that he would have preferred it if they had condemned *The End of the Affair*. 'Of course,' he said, 'you and I receive no harm from the erotic passages, but the young . . .' I told him, and it was true enough, though I had forgotten the evil influence of Sir Lewis Morris, that one of my earliest erotic experiences had been awoken by *David Copperfield*. Our interview at that point came abruptly to an end, and he gave me, as a parting shot, a copy of a pastoral letter which had been read in the churches of his diocese, condemning my work by implication. (Unfortunately I thought too late of asking him to authograph it.)[7]

'Haphazard' in the first sentence prepares us for the preference expressed by Cardinal Griffin. Which of one's novels with religious themes is banned by the Church depends, the writing implies, on the taste of the Cardinal who happens to be responsible for fiction. The tone of 'Cardinal Griffin remarked' sounds informal and so points out the oddness of the situation: 'remarked' suggests a personal preference mentioned in casual conversation. The note of gentle amusement is preserved in 'evil influence', of the harmless verses of Sir Lewis Morris and *David Copperfield*, 'parting shot', of a pastoral letter, and 'unfortunately' of a mischievous *esprit d'escalier*. In another account of the incident Greene extracts two formulae from the letter from Rome: the novel was condemned because it was 'paradoxical' and 'dealt with extraordinary circumstances'. These terms are nicely chosen: summarising central characteristics of Greene's work, and so implicitly condemning the whole *œuvre*, they are diverting, as strictures from a Cardinal – they might equally apply to the story of the Passion. That thought would not have diverted Cardinals Griffin and Pizzardo. When Pope Paul VI told Greene he had read *The Power and the Glory* and was told in reply that he had read a forbidden book, he smiled at the name Pizzardo.[8]

'Holiness and literary appreciation don't always go together,' one fictional bishop, in the first chapter of *Monsignor Quixote*, says of another, who disapproves of *Don Quixote*: 'a novel with many disgusting passages which in the days of the Generalissimo would not even have passed the censor.' Holiness and comic sense do not always go together either. It may be that true holiness lies beyond comedy. Churchmen of this sort are marked by unsmiling worldliness rather than holiness, in Greene. The disagreeable and humourless young priest Father Herrera, in *Monsignor Quixote*, is obviously destined for a bishopric. Such men can be sinister. 'The Generalissimo' tends to be a figure of fun in that gentle, late novel, set in Spain after Franco's death. In *The Honorary Consul*, bishops and would-be bishops are supporters of 'the heavy rule' of General Stroessner of Paraguay. This, rather than eroticism in English novels, is evil, Greene contends, and men such as Griffin ignore it. Greene's disapproval of the Church's right-wing influence in such parts of the world distinguishes him from Evelyn Waugh, a 'Catholic writer' who was much less willing to let the Church come within his sense of the ridiculous. Waugh would have preferred it if the Holy Office had condemned *A Burnt-Out Case*, a novel which makes cruel fun of characters who are stupid, inhumane and 'good Catholics'. Where they differ in this respect there is a solemnity and pomposity in Waugh which is alien to Greene.

Unhappiness at school is the key to Greene's interpretation of himself, and the conventional English public-school master is a figure in his personal myth at the opposite extreme from his outlook on life. He became, early in his schooldays, and remained for years, a skilled truant, hiding in hedges with a book, and he sees himself as a lifelong truant with a sympathy for all grown-up truants from the world of the well-behaved. Much could be made of the fact that his headmaster at Berkhamsted School was his father. He writes affectionately of Charles Greene, although with amusement at schoolmasterly traits: 'my father . . . once allowed his senior boys to go . . . for a special performance of the first Tarzan movie, under the false impression that it was an educational film of anthropological interest, and ever after he regarded the cinema with a sense of disillusion and suspicion'; 'I remember my father naming some place in France visited many years before and saying to [the friend with whom he took annual holidays], "You remember, George, that was where we drank a bottle of wine."'[9] He must have reflected that a man with a better eye for the incongruous would have noticed sooner that his son was willing to attempt suicide rather than face a new term.

Greene has related those unhappy early years to the two central precepts of his critical writing. In 'The Young Dickens' he says that 'the creative writer perceives his world once and for all in childhood and adolescence [so that] his whole career is an effort to illustrate his private world in terms of the great public world we all share'.[10] In another essay, 'Walter de la Mare's Short Stories', he says that every creative writer worth our consideration, every writer who can be called in the wide eighteenth-century use of the term a poet, is a victim: 'a man given over to an obsession'.[11] The opening two pages of *The Lawless Roads*, his travel book about Mexico, recreate a crucial moment from Greene's earliest perceptions of his world. He remembers himself at thirteen, 'alone in mournful happiness in the dark', hiding between the two adjacent realms of home and school.

> Two countries just here lay side by side. . . . You had to step carefully: the border was close beside your gravel path. . . . If you pushed open a green baize door in a passage by my father's study, you entered another passage deceptively similar, but none the less you were on alien ground. . . . How can life on a border be other than restless. You are pulled by different ties of love and hate.

The danger, fear and, sometimes, excitement of the mentality of a 'border' leading to alien ground are evoked again in *A Sort of Life*. *The Lawless Roads* finds the origin of Greene's religious belief in his sense of God at the moment of 'mournful happiness' alone and safe in the dark, 'And so faith came to one – shapelessly, without dogma, a presence above a croquet lawn, something associated with violence, cruelty, evil across the way'. Thirty years later, *A Sort of Life* is equally insistent:

> Years later when I read the sermon on hell in Joyce's *Portrait of the Artist* I recognised the land I had inhabited. I had left civilisation behind and entered a savage country of strange customs and inexplicable cruelties: a country in which I was a foreigner and a suspect, quite literally a hunted creature, known to have dubious associates. Was not my father the

headmaster? I was like the son of a quisling in a country under occupation.[12]

It may be objected that Greene's experience was not unusual. Many writers of his generation have protested about their schools: among those closest in age, Cyril Connolly (born 1903; Greene was born in 1904), in *Enemies of Promise*; Evelyn Waugh (born 1903), in *A Little Learning*; and Anthony Powell (born 1905), in *Infants of the Spring*, have described what Powell calls 'the disenchantments of schooldays'. Their schooling was particularly grim because of the rationing and irregular staffing caused by the war. But bookish children in any period are likely to react against the overcrowding and wasted time at school, and the noisiness of schoolboys and schoolmasters. Many of them bus or cycle across the border from a more civilised country every schoolday. For Greene, none the less, these years are the source of his obsessions: with evil and especially betrayal, savage countries, and the fears and excitements of the border, 'the dangerous edge of things' first known at the green baize door.

A Sort of Life tells us that Greene started a novel set in a school, in the late 1950s, and visited Berkhamsted to find little changed.

> I abandoned the novel – I couldn't bear mentally living again for several years in these surroundings. A leper colony in the Congo was preferable so I went to Yonda in search of a burnt-out case.[13]

Although the world of school was too horrible for treatment at length, many characters in the novels are haunted by thoughts of school and schoolmasters, or schoolboys who can be even more disagreeable. There is often a sad humour in observing how such memories linger, especially in the English, and how bizarre discrepancies appear between the standards of school and those of adult life. 'I was never a prefect, and the marbles team was the only one I ever made,' confesses Charley Fortnum, the consul in *The Honorary Consul*. 'Not recognised officially. We were a snobbish school,' (2.1). Another novelist (Powell, perhaps) might have made such a jest against the character, but Greene is firmly on the side of marbles against house-colours –

games, he recalls, were not those organised by adults – and Charley's rueful recollections of unsuccess at school, like those of Minty and Anthony Farrant in *England Made Me*, and Brown (a different sort of case) in *The Comedians*, arouse sympathy.

Schoolmasterliness takes various forms and occurs in characters who have avoided their true calling. Doctor Humphries in *The Honorary Consul* is a good example; he disapproves of Charley Fortnum and complains to the British embassy that the consul has flown the Union Jack upside down. Intellectuals can be as bad as such pedants, since Greene tends to share the view of Fortnum who says of his wife that 'she was an intellectual if you understand what I mean. She didn't understand human nature' (2.1). Another type of schoolmaster is the warder in *It's a Battlefield*, who boasts of his prison that it is 'just like a school' (1). A livelier comparison is made in *The Comedians* between school life and that of a brothel. Mère Catherine, who keeps the best 'house' in Haiti, is as punctilious as any headmistress but far more a mother to her girls. *A Sort of Life* makes the same connection. Sunday walks at Berkhamsted were organised in threes, lists being posted on a changing-room door. Greene comments that 'this surely must have had some moral object, though one which eludes me today when I remember how deftly the Emperor's Crown was performed by three girls at once in a brothel in Batista's Havana'.[14] Greene is not in favour of (or against) homosexual threesomes. He is against petty puritanical interference with others which belongs to those who put up such lists. 'Some moral object, though one which eludes me today' is one pose in which Greene affects to assume that the school authorities were familiar with the antics of Cuban prostitutes, and 'how deftly' is another, adopting the tone of a connoisseur and laughing at the authorities. But there is also amusement at himself: at the incongruity of memories which include Greene Minor looking resentfully at a list, and 'our man' in Havana. Cardinal Griffin would not have been amused and neither would the housemaster who censored Greene's reading at Berkhamsted.

Schoolmasterliness – or 'schoolmarminess' – in the derogatory sense of a narrow insistence on improving the young without understanding what they are really like can be seen in various characters in the novels: Mrs Bowles in *The Heart of the Matter* who says, 'We are not teaching the children to read in order that they shall read – well novels' (1.1.4); and the mother in *The Power and the Glory* who reads edifying hagiography to her yawning fourteen-year-old son. Greene's essay 'The Unknown War' (1940) introduces 'legendary figures of this war of whom most of us know nothing': Vulz, the mad German inventor, Billy the Penman, Worrals of the WAAFs, Captain Zoom, the Bird Man of the RAF. These heroes of the 'comics' *Rover, Hotspur* and *Boys' Own Paper*, are real in the minds of their readers: we say: 'How can anyone live with a child like that?' The answer, of course, is that he doesn't, except at mealtimes, live with *us*.'[15] Greene remembers and respects the intensity of childhood reading: 'the missed heartbeat, the appalled glee I felt when I found on a library shelf a novel by Rider Haggard, Percy Westerman, Captain Brereton or Stanley Weyman which I had not read before'.[16] There is, in Greene's novels, an allegiance to this aspect of childhood which mocks Mrs Bowles and all those who only read 'improving books', and is hostile to critics who try to make his novels more 'improving' than they are meant to be. If Greene is to be read in schools, he would prefer to be read under the desk.

Another figure alien to Greene is the successful man who values his success. John Buchan, for example, whom he admires for the adventure stories, 'repels' by 'the vast importance Buchan attributed to success', 'the Scotch admiration of success'. In the same article, 'The Last Buchan' (1941), he reflects that 'it is not after all the great men – the bankers and the divisional commanders and the Ambassadors who have been holding our world together this winter, and if we survive it is by the "wandering, wavering grace of humble men" in Bow and Coventry'.[17] A later essay, 'The Soupsweet Land', which is printed last as a 'Personal Postscript' in *Collected Essays* recalls his years in West Africa and especially the City Hotel in Freetown, Sierra Leone:

> There one escaped the protocol-conscious members of the secretariat. It was a home from home for men who had not encountered success at any turn of the long road and who no longer expected it . . . they were failures, but they knew more of Africa than the successes who were waiting to get transferred to a smarter colony and were careful to take no risks with their personal file.[18]

He felt at home there, disliking protocol, respecting those who knew more of the real country and took risks. On revisiting Freetown he went there again and, staying at a more confortable hotel, felt 'the guilt of a beach-comber *manqué*: I had failed at failure'. He ends by asking how the denizens of the City bar could 'tell that for a writer as much as for a priest there is no such thing as success?'[19] Here and in many other passages in autobiographical writing, he dignifies failure and claims a natural affinity.

A different account of his life might have made it seem a success story. After an especially dramatic flight from school he was sent to a psychoanalyst and returned, feeling worldly and distinguished, to read Browning, Swinburne, de la Mare, Racine and Strachey, in the relative freedom of the sixth form, and to go up to Balliol in 1922. At Oxford he won a minor scholarship, published a book of verse, edited a student paper, and took a Second in history. After a spell on a Nottingham newspaper, he was for three years a sub-editor on *The Times*, where, he admits, he was happy. He married (as a Catholic, received in 1926) and published *The Man Within*, his third completed novel, in 1929. His publishers offered him £600 a year to write three more novels in the next three years and he left *The Times*. *The Man Within* sold 8000 copies. The next two attempts were failures but his thriller *Stamboul Train* was chosen by the English Book Society. He made his name as a film critic for the *Spectator* and as a very lively, readable reviewer of books ranging from Beatrix Potter to Henry James. A trek through Liberia in 1935 produced one travel book, *Journey Without Maps*, and a journey through Mexico in 1938 another in *The Lawless Roads*. He edited the very distinguished although short-lived magazine *Night and Day*, wrote several more novels, finishing, before starting war-service (mostly in the secret service, in West Africa), *The Power and the Glory* which made him the best-known British novelist of his generation and, in the opinion of many reviewers of post-war novels, the best. He became a leading foreign and war reporter representing various papers, in Vietnam during the French struggle to hold the country, Malaya during the British effort against the Communists, Kenya during Mau Mau, Haiti, and in many other parts of the world. He became further known for plays (including *The Living Room*, produced in London, 1953; and *The Potting Shed*, produced in New York,

1957), screenplays (including *The Third Man*, with Carol Reed, 1950), biography (*Lord Rochester's Monkey*, 1974), criticism (*Collected Essays*, 1969), and editions (notably *The Bodley Head Ford Madox Ford*, 4 vols, 1962, 1963). He was made a Companion of Honour in 1966 and received the Order of Merit in 1985.

Much more might be said of his successes. Greene boasts of different achievements: combat with Papa Doc and with the Cardinals; successful truancies, and undergraduate escapades including a weird flirtation with the German secret service; free beer earned at *The Times* during the General Strike (before he became interested in politics); foiling official attempts to make him wear uniform during the war; conviction by the King's Bench for libelling the child-actress Shirley Temple (he wrote in *Night and Day* that there was deliberate coquetry, titillating to middle-aged men, in the waggling of her bottom); being deported from Puerto Rico by the Americans; praising Castro in public in Stroessner's Paraguay; representing Panama at a reception in Washington; and finding a friendly brothel in Corrientes after Argentina had made them illegal. He recounts such incidents with a cheerful pride in small acts of rebellion and amusement at taunting the 'protocol-conscious members of the secretariat'. He is of the Establishment but not for it. His orthodox forms of success, approved by the secretariat, are belittled. His minor scholarship at Balliol, he says, was arranged by his tutor, a family friend. He was unfortunate enough to have his poems published. A second-class honours degree is not a distinction at Oxford, but it is respectable (and a better result than his contemporaries Waugh and Powell achieved); Greene declines to have been respectable. He insists he was drunk during one whole term and driven by boredom in vacations to playing Russian roulette (a story not everyone believes).[20]

Greene is laconic and deprecating when he writes of his literary achievements. If we believe the tales rather than the teller, the growing enjoyment of story-telling and imaginative power, then the pleasure Greene derived from writing his novels is obvious. Even a novelist of saintly modesty might have been a little pleased by many of the reviews – if not the critical studies – of his work. But Greene dwells on the sense of failure. At school he wrote 'the most sentimental fantasies in bad poetic prose'. One particularly 'abominable story' was published in a local newspaper (three guineas paid).

Now, I told myself, I really was a professional writer, and never again did the idea hold such excitement, pride and confidence; always later, even with the publication of my first novel, the excitement was overshadowed by the knowledge of failure, by awareness of the flawed intention. But that sunny afternoon I could detect no flaw in *The Tick of the Clock*. The sense of glory touched me for the first and last time.[21]

That note of regret, for the greater novelist he might have been, is characteristic of the Introductions to the novels. *A Sort of Life* reports the feeling of triumph when *The Man Within* was accepted by Heinemann but immediately rebukes it: 'very young and very sentimental'.[22] Accounts of the subsequent years stress his difficulties. Greene does admit that he wanted to succeed as a writer, attributing his determination to the sting of failure during the unhappy years at school. The artistic and commercial failure of his second and third published novels *The Name of Action* and *Rumour at Nightfall* saved him, he says, from overwriting, in too lush a style, and taught him to draw upon 'my own experience, against the memories of flight, rebellion and misery during those first sixteen years when the novelist is formed'.[23] Relative success, when his style was pruned and personal experience tapped, is only grudgingly conceded: 'I can remember passages, even chapters which gave me at the time I wrote them a sense of satisfaction – this at least has come off. So I felt, however mistakenly'; he had 'at least once a momentary illusion of success'.[24] *A Sort of Life* ends with thoughts on the inevitability of a writer's sense of failure, in a report on a visit made in the 1950s to Thailand – then Siam – where a friend who had abandoned creative writing consoled himself with opium 'and an ironic amusement when he looked at his contemporaries who had found what people call success'.[25] Greene is quite happy to be the object of such amusement, and is amused himself by those who are not. They form another class apart in sympathy from the novelist who tends to celebrate those who have suffered what people call failure. So the doomed revolutionary Czinner, in *Stamboul Train*, is a better man than the best-selling novelist Savory; Minty, most degraded of remittance men, has the last word, in *England Made Me*; martyrdom is achieved by the whisky-priest in *The Power and the Glory*; the world-famous architect Querry flees from success in *A*

Burnt-Out Case and fails to get away; the unlucky confidence-man Jones in *The Comedians* and the whisky-consul in *The Honorary Consul* are sympathetic figures of fun; the 'poor monsignor errant' in *Monsignor Quixote*, though very vinous, limited in his priestly scope, and prone to doubt, is the sort of priest Greene would cheerfully drink with. There are vicious failures in the novels and a few characters who are successful and attractive; but the sense of failure always adds a dignity however slight and precarious. 'Sing of human unsuccess', Auden instructed poets who wanted to write in tune with their times.[26] Greene has sung of it consistently.

To be 'indifferent', in the sense of neutral and uncaring, is worse than to be shamelessly successful. Indifferent characters in the novels are often American, and an elderly American encountered in Mexico epitomises the condition. He shocked the young Greene because he was an untroubled and undoctrinaire non-believer – one for whom religion meant nothing. Greene can respect an atheist because that is a belief and one which needs courage.[27] Having been close to death during an illness this 'old gentleman from Wisconsin' had felt no emotion at the prospect, Greene reports, and comments indignantly: 'the old, good, pink face disclosed the endless vacancy behind'. They were equally estranged, as temporary travelling companions, by the American's inability to understand why one might prefer to walk about a foreign city rather than use a street-car. '"But I like walking," I kept on telling him – uselessly. "I'm going to tell them back home," he said, "about my English friend who walked all day and saved five cents American".' The revolutionary struggle in Mexico and the persecution of the Catholic Church held no interest to this tourist, who sought out fellow Americans and talked about his bowels: 'it might have been a dog speaking'.[28]

A certain rancour about England – and disinclination, especially in recent years, to live in it – arises partly from widespread English indifference to Greene's two great 'causes' of Catholicism and Communism, which the novels usually present as the only two options for a serious mind. During the 1930s when so many English writers were, or believed themselves to be, Communists, his Catholicism restrained him from joining the extreme left but there is an interest in the mystique of the Communist Party, and an insistence on the 'corruption' of capitalism, in the novels from *Stamboul Train* in 1932 to *Monsignor Quixote*, much of which is a friendly debate between a Catholic and a Communist, published fifty years later. It can be argued that Greene has dreamed of a Communism that does not and could not exist, and that if he were frank he would confess to the liberalism which marks all his work. Reporting a visit to Poland made in 1956, he discusses the Polish Catholic group *Pax*, which was supported by the authorities and therefore suspected by most Poles. Catholicism and Communism are closest, here, to an attempt at constructive coexistence; Greene sounds distinctly liberal, challenging representatives of *Pax* to declare their 'point of resistance', and regretting the 'political' phrasing introduced in the Pax catechism.[29] When a Polish newspaper reviewing *A Burnt-Out Case* welcomed the novel as an act of apostasy, Greene wrote to deny it and asked that a fee for quotations be paid to Warsaw Cathedral.[30] Greene is opposed to Communism as it exists, but respects Communists as far as he can see them as idealists, more aware of social evil than are the complacent majority of people. He deliberately overlooks what is logically untenable in this position, perhaps because Communism attracts him as a desperate faith held by its most intelligent adherents in spite of appearances.

Communism in Greene's imaginative worlds stands for a commitment to making the best of this world; if that is quixotic, he would accept the term. Catholicism represents serious religion. Anglicans and other Protestants tend to be mocked. (Buddhists are not: Greene used to pray to Buddha in their temples in the Far East, because 'now surely he is among our saints'. He reflects approvingly that Buddha, after all, failed.[31]) Non-Catholic clergy are seen as suburban, bourgeois, middlebrow and, worst of all, comfortable. When in *Stamboul Train* the desperate Czinner seeks confession, *faute de mieux*, from an Anglican parson, he gets a cosy chat in cricketing metaphors. Greenean religion is at its mildest, in *Monsignor Quixote*, uncomfortable. C. S. Lewis's spiritual autobiography is *Surprised by Joy*. Greene's, if he wrote one, might substitute 'Dread'. He has often been compared to the seventeenth-century Jansenists, somewhat heretical Catholics who emphasised the completely mysterious workings of the divine grace which alone can save us from hell. Some of Greene's most characteristic notions derive from Pascal, the leading Jansenist: 'sometimes we have a kind of love for our enemies and sometimes we feel hate for our friends'; and 'a ruined house is not miserable', which means that we should be proud of misery.[32] Greene admits to doubts about the doctrine of hell, but at least two of his characters, Pinkie in *Brighton Rock* and Scobie in *The Heart of the Matter*, are on the brink of it at the end of the novels in which they appear, and in *The Honorary Consul* the heretical priest turned revolutionary is in fear of damnation throughout; he tries desperately to confess and grant absolution to the apathetic consul whom he fears he will have to kill. To agonise over the difficulty of believing in hell is proper in Greene. It is ridiculous to be indifferent or glibly dismissive about this most dangerous 'edge of things'.

There is a sort of progress in, and perhaps out of, the faith to be charted in the autobiographical writings. Its instinctive origin lay in the horrors of school. Conversion, at twenty-one, was purely on grounds of intellectual conviction; Greene sought instruction, at first, only because he was to marry a Catholic. He became emotionally excited by his religion after witnessing the persecution of the Church in Mexico: the sanctus bell hushed for fear of the police; God smuggled into prisons in the pockets of schoolboys; the old Archbishop put over the border with only his breviary – 'the dangerous man'. *The Power and the Glory* grew out of these images, and despite condemnation, it is a novel written unambiguously in the cause of the Church. The reputation as a Catholic guru which arose in the 1950s brought numbers of unhappy Catholics, including priests, to consult Greene; he became conscious of faith as a storm at sea rather than a haven, and resented the role forced on him.[33] He grew doubtful himself; conditions in his private life estranged him from confession and communion until he found himself in 'the foreign legion of the Church'. But he considers the 'foreign legion' better than 'the suburbs' where sanctimonious intellectual believers 'have ceased to look for Him because they consider they have found Him'.[34]

Two modern Catholic writers Greene admires influenced his thought in at least a few of the novels. Charles Péguy (1873–1914), who is praised in *The Lawless Roads* for 'challenging God in the cause of the damned', was a socialist conscious of a world ruined by money, of socialism ruined by politicians, and of a church ruined by worldliness. He was in constant trouble with his political party and with other Catholics. Defeat and 'abandonment' are keys to salvation in his work (*A nos amis: à nos abonnés*, 1909; *Le Mystère de la Charité de Jeanne d'Arc*, 1910). Miguel de Unamuno (1864–1936), Professor of Greek and periodically, when not dismissed or banished, Rector of the University of Salamanca, was a Spanish Republican (who condemned both sides in the Spanish Civil War and died under house arrest) and a dissident Catholic. Greene found his *The Tragic Sense of Life* (1921) and other books appealing in their paradoxes, which make despair and disbelief the only sure ways to hope and faith.[35] Unamuno's novel *Manuel Bueno: Martir* (1933) is the story of an unbelieving priest. These men lived stormy but resolute political and religious lives far removed, to Greene's approval, from the complacencies of the 'suburbs'.

'Innocence' is an ambiguous term in Greene. Innocents touched by saintliness or true quixotry are attractive. But innocence is dangerous, even in children, as the excellent short story 'The Destructors' shows. Grown-ups have no right to it: they should know the world is a battlefield and a spiritual battlefield where evil is overwhelming. They can be preposterously funny, as is the judge who castigated *Night and Day* as a 'beastly publication' because of Greene's article about Shirley Temple. In different circumstances they are sinister, as is the American encountered in Vietnam who talked about a 'third force' to solve the war between Asian Communism and French colonialism, and who was the origin of the catastrophic innocent Pyle, in *The Quiet American*. Greene often reverses the sentimental interpretation of the teaching that only those who become like little children will enter the Kingdom. (Catholic exegesis on this text in Matthew 18.3 recommends humility rather than other childlike qualities.) Those who bring immature optimism to adult responsibilities are more likely to serve hell, however good their intentions; the boyish Pyle is an unconscious destructor. The plans of the CIA, which he represents, are childish. Both would be purely comic in a safe setting, but are tragi-comic in post-war Vietnam.

Greene follows Henry James in depicting innocent Americans among experienced, relatively corrupt old-worlders. His English are also prone to dangerous innocence, although he is ambivalent on this subject. Discussing English reactions to the insurgency

in Kenya in the 1950s he contrasts Mau Mau and the pure
pastoral of P. G. Wodehouse.

> It was as though Jeeves had taken to the Jungle. Even worse,
> Jeeves had been seen crawling through an arch to drink on
> his knees from a banana-trough of blood; Jeeves had transfixed
> a sheep's eye with seven kie-apple thorns; Jeeves had had
> sexual connection with a goat; Jeeves had sworn, however
> unwillingly, to kill Bertie Wooster 'or this oath will kill me
> and all my seed will die'.[36]

Catholic missionaries, he goes on to say, understand paganism
better than English settlers. In the novels, Catholicism gives a
common humanity to Englishmen who would otherwise be cut
off by their innocent integrity. When the Portuguese sea-captain
in *The Heart of the Matter* learns that Scobie is a Catholic he tries
to bribe him and this is a 'compliment'. The English colonial
police in the same novel are simpletons in comparison with the
Syrian traders whose wiles they can never detect. Father Rank
speaks of them 'carrying their happy morning faces around,
just going to pounce ... pounce on air' (2.1.2): these are
harmless innocents; Shakespeare's schoolboy's 'shining morning
face' is at the back of Father Rank's mind. The ordinary
middle-class life known to most of his English readers is
distasteful to most Greene characters who know the world.
Brown's mother, living in Haiti in *The Comedians*, asks 'And
how is England?' – 'as though she were enquiring after a
distant daughter-in-law for whom she did not greatly care'
(1.3.3). Greene knows England better and feels more affection
for Berkhamsted and Nottingham, but he suspects those who
only England know. They may remain trapped in their
childhood insecurities, like the murderous immature Pinkie,
child of the slums. Or they may assume that suburban England
is *real* life: such a man at the start of *Travels With My Aunt* is
Henry Pilling whose aunt educates him in smuggling and
resettles him in Paraguay. Such people, Greene complains,
cannot distinguish one of his foreign settings from another and
label them all 'Greeneland', a country of the mind.

The label was first publicised by Arthur Calder-Marshall in
a review article in *Horizon* in 1940.[37] One of Greene's defences

against those who deprecate the journalistic accuracy and range
of his novels is to point out that the real world imitates them.
Several reviewers of *The Honorary Consul* objected to the
predictability of setting, plot and roles. The fact that the leader
of the gang of leftists who kidnap the consul is a priest seemed
to them to confine the story to 'Greeneland'. Greene notes that
a British ambassador was kidnapped in Montevideo while he
was finishing his novel. The ambassador later reported that one
of his kidnappers was a priest. Francis Hope's review which
proposes that the novel was composed by a computer fed with
conventions from the earlier books, so that it is true only to its
own laws, concludes that 'people who like his sort of thing
should find this, quintessentially, the sort of thing they like'.[38]
Greene's report on his visit to Corrientes, in search of the
novel's setting, claims to be a fair sample of everyday life in
northern Argentina.

> Certainly my friends in Buenos Aires had exaggerated the
> dullness of Corrientes. In my first week there had been the
> abortive kidnapping, the expulsion of the third world priest
> from his church, the arrest of the Archbishop, the murder
> near the airport, and a few days after that a small and
> unimportant bomb was discovered in the cathedral.[39]

'Small and unimportant' puts Corrientes in perspective. Had
these been the events of a novel, the blend of church and crime
would have seemed, to some readers, true only to Greene's
fictional laws. He claims to ground his imagined worlds in the
familiar one: 'Greeneland perhaps: I can only say that it is the
land in which I have passed most of my life'.[40]

Another figure with whom Greene is out of sympathy is the
literary 'purist', most fully portrayed in the person of the
novelist of 'machismo', Doctor Saavedra, another innocent, in
The Honorary Consul. He condemns, by implication, the novel in
which he appears.

> If you were a writer, Doctor Humphries, instead of a teacher
> of literature, you would know a novelist has to stand at a
> distance from his subject. Nothing dates more quickly than
> the immediately contemporary. You might as well expect me to
> write a novel about the kidnapping of Charley Fortnum. (4.2)

Saavedra makes it his duty, in order to study the life of the poor, to visit the town's brothel once a week, but he explains that a writer 'has to transform reality'. The brothel girls are too beautiful for the 'bleak severity' of his fiction, and their beauty makes even their violation conventional. 'Pretty girls were being violated all the time everywhere, especially in the books of his contemporaries.' He therefore deprives one heroine of an eye, another of a leg, the eyeless girl being a 'Cyclops symbol' and the other a symbol of 'this poor crippled country'. 'A girl with one leg could be more easily violated', observes Doctor Plarr, his audience in the scene at the brothel where Saavedra lays down the literary law while Teresa, his girl for the evening, waits; but Plarr has 'little idea of how a writer's imagination works'. The novel about the one-legged girl is written. Doctor Plarr later visits Teresa himself and is 'amused to observe how far fiction deviated from reality. It was almost a lesson in the higher criticism' (2.2). When Plarr asks Saavedra for his signature to an urgent letter to *The Times* appealing for action to save the consul, the novelist refuses because he dislikes the style, and insists that he be allowed time to rewrite it. Then he finds himself defeated, in trying to evoke Charley's character, by his 'reality'. 'I am hamstrung by his reality' (4.2).

There is an element of self-mockery in this portrait. Greene has said that in drawing from life one must always change something. And Saavedra sounds rather like Greene when he says that he writes for the same reason the consul drinks, 'to escape the darkness of his own spirit' (4.2). Greene has complained that real-life models for fiction cramp his imagination.[41] But he wants us to feel that his character is absurd in missing both the comicality of his pose and its inadequacy. Saavedra defends his neglect of current affairs with the argument that Shakespeare did not deal with the political events of his own time; elsewhere Greene has attacked Shakespeare (very unreasonably) for neglecting to do so.[42] Saavedra is afraid to write about the 1970s because, like Shakespeare, he aims at posterity. For Greene the world is now so close to the dangerous edge of things that posterity has lost its appeal to a modern writer. Saavedra is most ludicrous in his failure to see the fictional possibilities in the plight of the kidnapped consul. He could not write, or appreciate, the novel in which he appears.

Greene's targets in life belong to his non-readers, if 'readers' means those who read with appreciation. Papa Doc and the Cardinals are extreme cases of antipathy. Charles Greene, who died in 1942, presumably read his son's earlier novels, but it is likely that they worried him. John Buchan, admirer of success, might well have agreed with Arthur Calder-Marshall who objected that Greene was obsessed with failures.[43] The American advocate of a third force in Vietnam is unlikely to have appreciated *The Quiet American*. Such a man as Greene's quiet American would have been baffled by the novel, if he had thought it worth his notice. Like Pyle, the innocents, indifferent and smugly successful characters in the novels are, even when relatively intelligent, completely out of tune with the point of view of their fictional worlds. Mr Smith would be pained by *The Comedians*. Ida Arnold would think *Brighton Rock* horribly morbid. Mr Savory would not approve of *Stamboul Train*; J. B. Priestley, who saw himself in that character, was not amused, and threatened to sue the publishers. Such a Spanish bishop as Monsignor Quixote's would, reading Greene, sigh for the days of the Generalissimo and his censors. A Rycker would think *A Burnt-Out Case* an insult to the Faith. Doctor Saavedra is, perhaps, a caricature, but most of us have known a Doctor Humphries; he would read *The Honorary Consul* without a smile.

Unsmiling, these types of people are deficient also in a tragic sense of life. Always fully alive to that sense, Greene has gradually developed a comic art which rarely forgets the tragic aspect of what is found amusing. 'Laughter in the shadow of the gallows' is a critical formula for *Travels with my Aunt* which Greene has approved; it would be apt for all the best late novels.[44] Commenting on his fiction in relation to his religion, Greene says that 'at the end of a long journey, without knowing myself the course which I had been taking, I found myself, in "A Visit to Morin" and *A Burnt-Out Case*, in that tragi-comic region of la Mancha where I expect to stay'.[45] Explicitly set in that region, *Monsignor Quixote* celebrates doubt as the essential condition of a healthy mind. That it is dreadful to be sure of oneself seems to be one of many of Greene's last words on his own work. His adversaries are not doubtful and, where they figure in the novels, that can be tragic or comic or, most effectively, both. He triumphs over them in his writing, asserting against their complacency his ironic, tragi-comic sense of life.

But on the question of whether novels can make any impact on the indifferent, falsely innocent, success-seeking, schoolmasterly world, not everyone among those who most appreciate Greene will agree.

2

Early Novels

The best of the earliest novels show that Greene's comic gift is as strong as his gift for the macabre; when they are most effective, they show creative relations between the two. They also imply a suspicion of comedy, especially when it consoles or screens the worst aspects of life. The tragedy of Europe in the 1930s, the Depression and the rise of Fascism, is never forgotten in these books. The first of them, *Stamboul Train* (1932), mixes comic scenes with disasters, and sets innocent and complacent English characters against a background of tragedy to which the eastern-European hero belongs. *It's a Battlefield* (1934) insists unremittingly on the ghastly fates of its characters; its only jokes are deliberately unfunny. *England Made Me* (1935), also emphatically indignant, is a better book for its mournful comedy, although no less pessimistic than the earlier novels, or those which were to follow.

Stamboul Train was Greene's first fully successful novel.[46] He wrote it to make money and gave it the subtitle 'An Entertainment'; it sold well and it still entertains. Like many of his books, it is a sort of thriller, among other things. Greene says that the thriller chose him rather than he the genre, and the hero of the wartime novel *The Ministry of Fear* argues that 'spies, and murders, and violence, and wild motor-car chases' have become, since 1914 when stable, peaceful England ended, 'real life': 'what we've all made of the world'. 'The world, he says, 'has been remade by William Le Queux' (5.1).[47] A lifelong taste for the conventions and spirit of adventure stories appears in Greene's fondness for remembering the Weymans and Buchans of his earliest reading, and in his first attempts at fiction. The second of his unpublished apprentice novels portrayed romantic figures from Carlist Spain; another, unfinished venture was a detective story about a governess murdered by her pupil – detected, but not given away, by a priest. *The Man Within* (1929), unashamedly romantic, is about a young smuggler on the run from the shipmates he has betrayed; like most of the novels, it ends in violent death. The second and third to be published (later suppressed and disclaimed), *The Name of Action* (1930) and *Rumour at Nightfall* (1931), turn on gun-running in Trieste and the Carlist War in Spain (where the author had once spent a day). When espionage and violence set the tone of political life in Europe in the 1930s, one aspect of Greene's taste in fiction was well-suited.

A world remade after the thrillers of William Le Queux is absurd, and farce offered an alternative metaphor for modern conditions, in the manic stories of Evelyn Waugh, for example. Thrillers can easily be travestied as farce and farce as light comedy can be darkened into the macabre. Greene says that he has always thought farce more akin to tragedy than comedy is.[48] The epigraph to *Stamboul Train* is a quotation from George Santayana: 'Everything in nature is lyrical in its ideal essence; tragic in its fate, and comic in its existence'. The story alternates and mixes tragedy and comedy, and sometimes creates a no-man's land between, too absurdly calamitous for either yet edging on both. It can be thought of as a farcical thriller, because it explores what farces and thrillers have in common. Both types of writing use swift reversals of situation and both rely on situation more than character, often using simple characters of familiar types. Both require narrative skill and economy in writing. Both are as strictly ruled by convention as games are; like all Greene's novels, both resemble games of hide and seek.

The Orient Express, London to Istanbul, was the most romantic of trains; *Stamboul Train* exploits one part of the romance, the poetry of foreign place-names, in the title and in the headings for the five parts: Ostend, Cologne, Vienna, Subotica, Constantinople. One of the novel's passengers has a false British passport and a purpose for travelling which might be thought worthy of the train, although he would not think it romantic. Dr Czinner is going to lead a revolution in Belgrade. He has been in hiding, during the five years since he fled from Yugoslavia, as 'the foreign master' at a private school. It is described to sound like Berkhamstead, but named, as though in a farce, Great Birchington-on-Sea. Now the militants are ready, and the poor of the slums where he practised medicine will rise in support when Dr Czinner is known to have returned.

A journalist, Miss Mabel Warren, spots him at the station in Cologne, where she has come to see off her companion – Janet Pardoe, another of the novel's cast – and to write a piece for her newspaper about the other celebrity on board the express, a best-selling novelist, Quin Savory. Scenting a scoop and partly drunk, she hauls herself into the moving train: 'Dizzy Mabel comes on board'. After the modest success of *The Man Within*, Greene had failed twice to produce a marketable novel and may well have felt some rancour against the authors of middle-. brow best-sellers. He makes unkind fun of Savory and should not have been surprised when J. B. Priestley, whose novel *The Good Companions* (1929) was one of the most remarkable middle-brow successes of the century, took offence. Savory's opus is *The Great Gay Round*, a title which summarises what Greene does not feel about life. The scene in which Miss Warren interviews him influences our reading of the graver issues of Europe in 1932 where Communist movements and Fascist countermovements are clashing. Hitler came to power in 1933.

> But one 'opes, one 'opes, that it's something of this sort, to bring back cheerfulness and 'ealth to modern fiction. There's been too much of this introspection, too much gloom. After all, the world is a fine adventurous place. (2.1)

His next book 'Going Abroad' is to be 'an adventure of the Cockney spirit'. In the process of making himself one of the masters of modern gloom, Greene evidently enjoyed putting this breezy innocent in his melancholy adventure story. With Dr Czinner we return to the novel's real world of spies and violence, which in Greene's presentation is dignified by failure. Czinner has learned from a newspaper bought in Cologne that the uprising has already taken place, three days before schedule and, without his name for a rallying cry, has been suppressed. Thinking of his ruined prospects, he tells himself 'with triumph "I am afraid"'. A characteristically abrupt change of scene and tone at the start of the next section (2.2), returns us to light comedy:

'Not *the* Quin Savory?' asked Janet Pardoe.

'Well,' said Mr Savory, 'I don't know of any other.'

'*The Great Gay Whirl?*'

'*Round*', Mr Savory corrected her sharply.

His self-importance sounds particularly smug after the triumph of fear.

Passages which trace Dr Czinner's pained thoughts continue to alternate with scenes of farce. He is drawn into absurd situations with the other passengers, rescuing the chorus girl Coral Musker who is squabbling with a shopkeeper's wife: 'No wonder your old man wanted a change. . . . He wouldn't soil his hands with you.' Meanwhile he tells himself that he has failed as a son because education has alienated him from his parents, as a doctor because his patients could never afford his prescriptions, and now, as a socialist. The sense of failure stirs his conscience and he worries about his mixed motives in travelling first class. As all other beliefs come into question, the Catholicism of his childhood, set aside on Marxist principle, gradually revives. He decides to look for a priest, which, ironically, brings him back into the world of farce.

The Reverend Mr Opie is Anglican, and hopelessly innocent. He is, he explains to Czinner, making a religious anthology which will give the Church of England something to replace Roman Catholic contemplative writing; it will serve 'deeper' English needs. He describes the type of crisis where spiritual comfort and strength might be required: last man in, with fifty runs to make. Czinner is baffled: 'he did not understand the words "pad", "wickets", "runs". The religious significance of the words escaped him' (3.1). He tries to explain that he wants to be confessed; Opie has admitted to being a priest although not Roman, and presumably Czinner has never fathomed what the Church of England is. Opie chats fair-mindedly about confession: there is a modern parallel in psychoanalysis. This is, perhaps, predictable malicious teasing by a formerly Anglican Roman-Catholic convert. But Opie's speeches are nimbly written. When he says that psychoanalysis may be more 'efficacious' than confession, the word makes his reasonableness sound prissy. When Savory joins them, Opie welcomes the prospect of 'a really interesting discussion', sounding just like a bland English parson. Savory proposes that a novelist's role is like that of a penitent, 'confessing for the public'. Opie does not spot the pun in Czinner's name, neither does he notice that the man is in trouble. This short, witty scene dramatises the distance between the middle-brow English culture of interesting discussions and eastern Europe (where Opie lives).

Events become more real for Dr Czinner when the train reaches the border at Subotica where Colonel Hartep, Chief of Police in Belgrade, has arranged for his arrest. If the company of Opie and Savory makes him almost comic in 'existence', with Hartep he is in company where another writer might have presented his fate as a dignified tragedy. Czinner has imagined himself a public hero in a courtroom in the capital, orating to the world before dying for his cause. Greene is more realistic. Nervous about what may be offered for lunch at a frontier barracks, Colonel Hartep has brought sherry, champagne, cold duck and other provisions whose welfare matters more to him than the routine summary trial, possible since martial law has been introduced, after which the would-be leader of the revolution is to be executed as soon as night falls. Smoothly articulate and competent, he is far more than equal to the local army commander's fuss about irregularities. The 'genuine kindness' he shows his prisoner disarms Czinner who is reduced to a 'tub orator', in Hartep's opinion at least, as he speaks of the brotherhood of man, his only listener, finally, the simple soldier Ninitch. A chance of escape, after sentence has been passed, preserves the adventure-story excitement, as do other events but Dr Czinner's end, farcical in the travesty of justice, is also so in the circumstances with which the novel surrounds it.

Two other passengers are arrested with Czinner. They are given light sentences but since the three try to escape together, under gunfire, there is thrillerish curiosity about what will happen to whom. A German criminal, Josef Grünlich (the surname means 'greenish'), boards at Vienna , having committed a murder when surprised during a burglary – all of which is described, to add to the impression of a violent world outside the train. Czinner closely escapes being shot by Grünlich who decides instead, when caught thieving, to pose as a socialist and is given five pounds. Other ironies connected with the burglar are more interesting than he is, including the last which is that

he alone succeeds in the escape attempt. In love with his gun
(and arrested for possession of it) and the use of it to 'spill the
guts' of anyone in his way, he is also dedicated to his reputation
as a crook who has never been caught. He makes an appropriate
bizarre companion for the doctor. So does Coral Musker, the
feeble-looking but resilient chorus girl to whom Czinner passes
a note to be posted, when he sees arrest coming, causing her to
be detained. Murder and Communism are equally shocking to
her, but that is because of her indifference rather than any
belief. She regrets that Czinner has never learned 'the only
way' in life which is 'not to fuss' and 'let things slide' (4.3).
Coral is not pretty, but she has attractive legs and two of the
other passengers compete for her.

Mr Carleton Myatt is a rich young merchant in currants,
very Jewish in his own mind and in the novel's presentation of
him in other ways; the menacing hatred in the cries of *'Juif!
Juif!'* with which he has to contend throughout his journey adds
to the sense of gathering storm. He pays for a first-class ticket
for Coral, sleeps with her and promises to make her his mistress,
a modest success which she finds too good to be true. His rival
is Miss Warren, who has been in love with Janet Pardoe, but
fears that this 'companion' will soon defect, as it were, to a
man. Greene treats his character's homosexuality with sympathy
for the suffering which it involves and mockery of its consolations.
She must have been even more bizzare to the average reader of
1932 than she is today. Carleton Myatt is too absorbed in
thoughts of business to notice Coral's disappearance at Subotica.
When, later, the engine fails, he hires a car to take him back to
her rescue, but by this time he has come to prefer Janet Pardoe,
whom Savory is courting. He shows resolve and courage, none
the less, in his pursuit of Coral, but is deceived by Grünlich on
the run, and returns to the train with the burglar instead.
Czinner has been fatally wounded in the escape and is tended
by Coral who is still full of thoughts of a rich life with Myatt.
Czinner's death is rendered at length and horrifically; the young
Ninitch, who Czinner has befriended, is ordered to blow out the
dead man's brains. Czinner dies in despair, having failed, he
believes, totally, since the world will know nothing of his fate. A
moment later Coral finds that it is not Myatt but Miss Warren
who has arrived to carry her off, and win her scoop, thus dizzily
uniting the climax of the thriller and the climax of the farce.

The newspapers and history will know of Czinner's Marxist martyrdom, but no official Communist history-book would acknowledge the full circumstances which have brought that about. The principal Soviet reference book in English which gives information about Greene does not mention his irony.[49]

The 1974 Introduction declines to see 'much promise' in *Stamboul Train*, or feel much in common with the young novelist. The habitual irony which leaves nothing alone, even the strength of feeling about social injustice, is what most strikingly contradicts both these subterfuges. Irony can be contrived, as it is when the purser looks at Czinner, in Ostend, and wonders 'whether something dramatic had passed close by him, something weary and hunted and the stuff of stories' (1.1). Sometimes it is heavy as in Grünlich's declaration to Czinner, 'I am a Socialist'. It is contrived and heavy when Grünlich realises in the first pleasure of his escape that the soldiers who have let Myatt's car go through the roadblock were looking for somebody they thought more important (he can't guess whom), and he sits 'brooding on the injustice of it all'. Some ironies are small, personal and idiosyncratic, such as the allusion to Greene's name in the murderer's. Other are large and public, part of the consciousness of the time. Such is the point, which helped to make frontiers so conspicuous in the literature of the period, that while aeroplanes have in one way 'abolished frontiers', it is becoming harder than ever to cross them in Europe afflicted by modern nationalism. Czinner, who pleads to Hartep that frontiers are things of the past, dies and is buried on one which will stay.[50]

Other twists in the story are related to ironic features of the period which were widely recognised in literature. Czinner and Coral sing to each other while they are locked up at Subotica. The old man's is a traditional folk song in which a lover and his girl arrange to evade her father and meet in the orchard at the bottom of the garden, 'a sad idyll' which draws the guards to listen, and the singer to forget his defeats and to think of the 'sad and beautiful' faces of his poor. Coral tries to recall something as 'old fashioned', to comfort him, but can produce only a song from a show.

> I was sitting in a car
> With Michael;

I looked at a star
  With John;
I had a glass of bitter
  With Peter
  In a bar;
But the pips went wrong; they never go right.
  This year, next year
(You may have counted wrong, count again, dear),
  Some day, never
I'll be a good girl for ever and ever.

The scene closes there without comment. Coral is one of the poor and young for whom Czinner has sacrificed himself, urging Hartep to stop protecting 'an old world which is full of injustice' and join the cause of the new, just one. This sort of optimism, in the 1930s, went uneasily with a fear among intellectuals that the popular culture had been permanently impoverished, or destroyed. The old man sings of romance in verses remembered from youth; the girl, though she wants to please him, sings of cynical infidelity, in a brand-new tissue of cheap phrases, which is all she has to remember.

Another 'public' irony bears on the English. The connotations of 'England' and 'English', for intelligent people of Greene's generation, changed from the unquestioning assurance of Empire instilled in childhood to equally vapid assumptions about 'late capitalism' when the Great War, followed by grave economic depression, thinned confidence. If the change was more thoughtful than plain disillusion, as it seems to have been for Greene, it was even more likely to sharpen an ironic cast of mind. 'But 'ow did you know I was English?' Savory asks Opie when they meet, and he replies, 'I make a practice of always thinking the best of people' (1.1). The silliness of this pronouncement is one of the novel's themes, and all the English characters illustrate its falsehood. One attraction of a train as a novel's setting is that it brings close people of many backgrounds and classifies them. Myatt, in the first class, is happy only in business calculations; he thinks of the English as an alien people, like Turks, with whom it is good to do business because his race makes them simpletons. Opie and Savory, in the second-class sleepers, are presented as bogus but typically

English representatives of priest and novelist. In the second-class non-sleeping compartments are the shop-keepers, called Peters, who rail that Coral is a 'tart' when Myatt rescues her from the cold: 'Yes, but who pays? That's what I'd like to know'. Czinner hisses at them, '*Bourgeois*'. An intrepid woman journalist might have been a heroine in a different sort of thriller, especially in the 1930s when the role had glamour; Miss Warren, usually half-drunk and day-dreaming of girls in pyjamas, sees in Czinner an extra four pounds a week, as a reward if she obtains her scoop, and her petty, mercenary mentality is, the novel implies, typically English.

The English characters can, like so many people in Greene, be seen as 'alienated', not just in being abroad, but in having left their original social class, or culture, or sexual role. Savory and Coral have moved upwards socially, he more than her. Both are displaced rather than reassigned. Using his dialect as a professional credential, Savory is uneasily conscious that people who do not know that he is a 'genius' just think him vulgar. Coral, who spends her life vainly trying to be like a lady, is astonished when Czinner admits his working-class origin. Opie is absurdly out of context, trying to spread cricket through Europe, a sort of missionary for the game. Miss Warren is as masculine as possible. But Czinner is alienated because *déclassé*, and it is in relation to him, and to Grünlich, the only other foreigner among the passengers who figure in the story, that the English are seen. In this contrast, Englishness is pictured as trivial because uncommitted. Czinner has his cause, and even better, in Greene's world, he fails and suffers in it. Grünlich crazily believes himself a great man: ominously, since he is a German, he dreams that he is President of the Republic. He is evil. *Brighton Rock* was to be inspired by Greene's belief that evil people are more real than commonplace 'innocents'. The beginnings of such an assertion can be seen in *Stamboul Train*. Far from thinking the best of people, Opie cannot imagine the quality of such a man as Czinner and that limitation seems connected with his blandness when he chats about cricket with Josef Grünlich.

There are further sad ironies at the expense of English assumptions of superiority to foreigners (there is a refrain of 'can't understand these foreigners' among the humbler characters from the start) in the final chapter, set in

Constantinople. Coral has intended to join Dunn's Babies, an English troupe of dancers currently performing at the Pera Palace. When Myatt has detached Janet Pardoe from Savory, and decided to marry her to consolidate a business deal with her uncle, Mr Stein, he takes her there. Dunn's Babies, dressed as railway guards except for their shorts, dance and sing, in the final pages.

> If you want to express
> That kind of gloom
> You feel alone in a double room.

Myatt is in the middle of an account of a girl's hysterical breakdown. Song lyrics comment like this in many of Greene's novels. This song, distinctly up-to-date in 1932 and now distinctly 'thirties', is appropriately glib for an after-dinner show, but the shallow hedonism is made to sound an expression of English culture, a sign of indifference, by the presence of a Turkish audience which includes (improbably) women only recently emancipated from veils. A sailor staggers drunk to the stage when the Babies sing 'Come up here', and collapses there. The audience laughs. There is always a ghastly note in public laughter in Greene. (In the courtroom scene in *The Man Within* the hero, asked where his father is, replies 'in Hell, I hope' and the court resounds with laughter.) The sailor, it is noted, is English.

Ironic juxtaposition in the novel's final paragraph shows Dunn's Babies in relation to the whole story in which violence mingles constantly with levity. As Myatt proposes to Janet,

> . . . Dunn's Babies stamped their feet and blew their whistles.

> 'Waiting at the station
> For a near relation,
> Puff, puff, puff, puff.'

Myatt said, 'Don't go back to her. Stay with me'.

> 'Puff, puff, puff, puff, puff.
> The Istanbul Train.'

She nodded and their hands moved together. He wondered whether Mr Stein had the contract in his pocket.

Most of the novels which were to follow end in death by
violence, not marriage. The mocking chorus to this unromantic
union recalls the journey, and so reminds us of the death of
Czinner, the climax to which the light comedy of this last
chapter is an ironic comment.

Stamboul Train is a book one might offer a young reader as an
introduction to Greene, with the promise of better, and more
problematic novels to come. Read today, it invites us to look
ahead to the mature novels which are creatively problematic in
their quandaries over the comic aspects of calamity. *It's a
Battlefield* is not likely to be anybody's favourite, and it is
untypical in the extent to which it mutes Greene's comic sense.[51]
The result is very bleak. All Greene's work implies the vanity of
worldly hopes of almost every kind, but humour represents a
resilience, which has helped to keep him writing during recent
decades, and which is largely absent here.

As a novel about 'the condition of England' in 1934, it evokes
the mood of the time in which so many intelligent people
became Communists, although the portrayal of Communists in
the novel is unlikely to have encouraged conversions. 'It' was a
battlefield, for Marxists, because of the class war; Greene's
theme is the inadequacy of all human justice, not only that of
capitalist society.[52]

One of the novel's ironies is that the Assistant Commissioner
of the London police, a major figure, intent on justice as an
administrator and (very improbably) in everyday police work,
does not believe in it. He sees himself, with dissatisfaction, as
an indifferent who has 'stood aside'. As he did when he was a
colonial police officer, burning villages in Asia, so now in
pursuit of London's criminals, he merely obeys his superiors –
politicians and judges. He disclaims personal responsibility. At
the end of the story he is half-inclined to resign because justice
seems so unjust, but his only satisfaction is in work and the last
paragraph leaves him still at work.

Other ironies make the plot a cruel, humourless farce. Jim
Drover, a bus driver, has been sentenced to hang for killing a
policeman who was, he thought, about to hit his wife, at a
Communist disturbance. Much of the story concerns attempts
to secure his reprieve, by petition or influence. His brother
Conrad, a chief clerk, becomes deranged after a night in bed

with his brother's wife Milly. After anguished wanderings through London, he is fatally injured by a skidding car, while trying to kill the Assistant Commissioner with a revolver loaded with blanks. Jim is reprieved. He at once attempts suicide at the prospect of eighteen years in prison, apart from the wife he loves. The prison chaplain, who has resigned as a result of this irony, because he can no longer stand human justice, tells the Assistant Commissioner in the last pages, that there is only one comfort for Jim: his devoted brother will look after Milly. The news then arrives that Conrad has died (after terrible suffering).

The name Conrad is no accident. It was given in tribute to a merchant navy officer who once lodged with the Drovers. It is a doubtful tribute on the novelist's part. Joseph Conrad was naturally an inspiration to him. Conrad had been the great modern artist of the story of action in exotic places, an ironist, a novelist of ideas, psychological subtlety and technical innovation. His influence is very conspicuous in this book, especially in the Assistant Commissioner, a thoughtful and practical bachelor whose face is yellow from a lifetime in the East, who sees into the evil of life but dutifully endures, solaced by his work, wanting to belong to the police and not merely head them. But Greene regretted the influence of Conrad on his second and third novels, and that of the untypical, romantic historical novel *Arrow of Gold* (1919) in particular, in causing him to write affected prose ('A clock relinquished its load of hours' is one of his examples) about romantic foreign places he had not visited. Greene is unashamedly superstitious about names, and Conrad Drover's fate may represent an attempt to exorcise Conrad – whom he for years forbade himself to read.[53] The novel was an exercise in realism, concentrating on misery in a realistic modern London, and intended to expel, or suppress, the demon of romantic self-indulgence.

The thought that hell, rather than a battlefield, makes an apt metaphor to summarise life occurs to the Assistant Commissioner when he visits the prison where Jim Drover awaits execution. A warder stresses the 'humane' system whereby prisoners are promoted from Block A via B to Block C where they have special privileges. 'It's just like a school', he says without intended irony, and it is made to sound so: 'every man to his cell except Block C'; 'they have an hour for reading before lights out'. The visitor recalls that Dante mapped Hell in circles, and tells himself that this is only an outer circle. The point that the outside world contains other kinds of prison is remorselessly imposed on the reader. Milly Drover's sister Kay works in a match factory which has a system of promotion for its workers; they rise from Block A via B to Block C, although, like the prisoners, they are demoted for mistakes. The novel shows life at its worst where it is modern. The Assistant Commissioner has seen men laughing together in the squalid prisons of colonial Asia; he has heard that men go mad in English prisons. The match factory is very efficient. Jim's job as a bus driver has minimised his interest in life. Asleep in his cell, he sits in the posture of a driver in the cab. His only sign of interest when mates are allowed to call is on hearing that a change has been made to the route of his bus. His brother finds work as a chief clerk unbearable, and regrets that he was born with 'brains'; he is haunted by memories of unhappiness at school. Milly goes to ask the widow of Jim's victim to sign the petition, and finds her to have eyes 'bewildered and hunted' (3). This reassures her because the widow's photograph in the newspaper had seemed 'harsh and unbearable'. Another character, Jules, is a waiter:

> 'You've forgotten the butter, Jules.'
> 'You've forgotten the sugar.'
> 'No knife, Jules.'

> The young man ran back and forth from his counter with a lost look like a dog taken shopping. (4)

'Too much gloom,' Mr Savory comments on modern literature, in *Stamboul Train*. Wanting as much gloom as possible, Greene has decided in this novel on a tone of monotonous gloom.

'Satanic laughter' is a term which G. Wilson Knight used in his essay, '*King Lear* and the Comedy of the Grotesque'.[54] C. S. Lewis explored the idea in *The Screwtape Letters*.[55] Writing in 1968 about Bernanos's *Sous le Soleil de Satan* (1926), Greene praises that novel's portrayal of a devil who appears 'in the guise of a little lubricious horse-dealer with his sinister gaiety and his horrible affection and his grotesque playfulness'. 'Infantility', he says, is a mark of hell, which appears in the infantile jokes of the devils in Marlowe's *Doctor Faustus*.[56] 'Sinister gaiety' and 'grotesque playfulness' are present throughout Greene's novels, and some critics have accused him of hankering for the devil's side.[57] But there would be no human gaiety or play in hellish laughter. It would be unfunny to us, as de Sade usually is; 'infantile' is the apt pejorative note. *It's a Battlefield* is full of such jokes and it ends, most unamusingly, in a spate of them; the injured Conrad, for example, tries to scream but cannot because his jaw is broken. One modern analyst of comedy, Moelwyn Merchant, has observed that 'farce may be transcended in a further horror – and here neither "comedy" nor "tragedy" are terms which fit the case'. Merchant gives as an example from Peter Weiss's *The Investigation* these lines about a wartime extermination camp:

> I myself
> only escaped gassing
> by accident
> because on that evening
> the ovens were clogged up.[58]

Irony, in these lines and even in Greene's point about a broken jaw, provides an affinity to humour. In the 'joke' which Conrad plays in the third part of *It's a Battlefield*, there is no such affinity. He goes into a gun shop and pretends that he wants to buy a revolver. (Greene seizes the chance to remind us of the idle rich in a background conversation about grouse-moors.) When the assistant has shown him various guns he admits that he has no licence and leaves. The 'joke', he regrets, is not funny enough to let him or Milly forget Jim in prison, and he reflects that if Jim is reprieved there will be 'a flat end to every story' for the next eighteen years. On a second reading of the novel, we notice these sentences:

> How long before one could laugh or smile? How long these cramped muscles of the mouth?

Such time-bombs of irony are a pleasing feature of Greene's art; this one, alluding to the broken jaw, is not intended to please.

Other episodes have flat endings in the sense of resembling jokes which fail, or comic possibilities which stay unused. The journalist Conder, who has various fantasy lives, cannot

persuade his colleagues to accept him in the romantic roles, but
they believe his talk about a wife and six children and the new
house, although Conder lives alone with a collection of foreign
coins. He might have been a comic figure, but is not. The
Assistant Commissioner takes part in a raid on the house of a
murderous member of the Salvation Army. When they arrive,
he is practising.

> I've been as big a sinner as any of you.
> But I've come to Jesus and been forgiven . . .
> Oh, if only you knew friends, the sweetness
> of that forgiveness, the balm, the peace.

He is a trunk-murderer, who left his victim's corpse cut up and
cased at Paddington Station. Evelyn Waugh would have enjoyed
the situation of such cant at the moment before the arrest:
Greene begins the joke and flattens it by emphasising at the
end of the scene ('You ought to be ashamed, hitting me') the
pity of the man's madness, as Waugh does not for the splendid
religious maniac who carves up Mr Prendergast in *Decline and
Fall*. Greene's salvationist may be remembered as an instance
of black comedy, but his scene closes in pure melancholy.

One character, Mr Surrogate, a rich Communist, does figure
in one of the lightest comic scenes in all the early novels. The
titles of the books he has written show his 'advance' towards
Marxism. *Forward to Free Trade* is the earliest and *No Compensation*
the most recent. One evening he hears a rustling behind the
copies on his shelf, and removes three editions of *No Compensation*.

> There, surprised in the act of dining, a nut between its paws,
> sat a mouse. Mr Surrogate and the mouse were both startled.
> For quite a while they stared at each other without moving.
> The mouse did not even drop a nut. Perhaps it hoped to
> remain unnoticed. It may never have seen before a human
> face so close, almost within reach of an extended tail, and the
> great white moony expanse may have had the appearance of
> a natural phenomenon. (2)

The last two words are a comic shift into an adult register
because the simple graceful prose is like the best writing for
young children. 'Surprised in the act of dining' is just right:

'dining' is a courteous beginning to the game of pretending that a mouse is like ourselves except in form; 'surprised in the act', as though of a crime, points out the discrepancy between our point of view and that of the trespassing mouse. 'Mr Surrogate and the mouse were *both* startled' puts a delicate stress on the difference of scale. Common speech tends to place 'before' after the adjective in the structure of 'never seen a human face so close before'; Greene's placing alters the rhythm and leaves 'close' uncluttered so that we notice the word. Noticing prepares us for the mouse's eye view of a human face. Mr Surrogate is sentimental. He remembers 'the great Russian novelist comforted in the Siberian prison by the nightly visitation of a mouse' and he thinks of 'the prison of this world'. He offers it toasted cheese. It declines to entertain him, however, hiding behind *The Capital Levy*.

It had a shiny rump and an air of great respectability. One expected a bunch of keys to dangle at the waist; but it preferred to eat in the housekeeper's room.

The keys and the housekeeper belong to the world of Beatrix Potter, much admired by Greene.[59] He enjoys linking thoughts of her with Dostoevsky in Siberia. But the fun of this passage is subordinated to the novel's tragic themes. Mr Surrogate notices that *The Dictatorship of the Worker* has been nibbled at and he orders a mousetrap. Comic in its existence the mouse is tragic in its fate. *It's a Battlefield* is a novel about mantraps.

If the mouse is connected with large themes in *It's a Battlefield*, *England Made Me* figures human affairs in the form of a spider which belongs to its central character Minty.[60] The spider is trapped under a glass in Minty's very shabby room in Stockholm, maimed and apparently doomed. When we meet it, it has been watching him for five days, 'with shaggy patience' (3.1). In a later scene he finds that he needs the glass because his landlady has broken his cup. The spider has shrivelled and seems dead. But after his cocoa, Minty finds that it was shamming.

It was cunning, not death, which had withered it; now blown

out to twice the size, it was dropping to the floor on its invisible thread.

The hunting instinct woke in Minty's brain; it had been a good day's sport. He took the glass and caught the spider . . . Patience, Minty thought, patience; you may outlive me. (3.5)

In the excitement of the spider Minty gets into bed without saying his prayers, but prays in bed: 'that God would cast down the mighty from their seats'; and that 'the Minister would consent to a Harrow dinner'. He thanks God for a 'happy and successful day', and he lies 'in darkness, like the spider patient behind the glass'.

And like the spider he withered, blown out no longer to meet contempt; his body stretched doggo in the attitude of death, he lay there humbly tempting God to lift the glass.

This section (3.5) is the core of the novel.

All the novel's characters live 'blown out' to meet the world; they are all shams, although unlike Minty and the spider they usually pretend to be more than they are. Anthony Farrant, the central character in the plot, is a shabby-genteel, unreliable drifter. Greene says that Anthony is a portrait of his elder brother, and he is presented with a blend of sympathy for his failure and reproach for his attempts to pose as a success.[61] He is cut off or 'alienated' from England and from the upper middle class in which he was unhappily educated at a minor public school. He wears the tie of the more prestigious Harrow. Minty is a Harrovian, and one of his roles is to spot the small fraud, and make the comment at the end which concentrates the novel's theme that modern Europe is a vast fraud. Another of Minty's roles is to illustrate the title's ironic point about how badly England has made the people who resemble the novel's main characters. When Anthony ran away from his school, always in Greene the right move, his twin sister Kate persuaded him to return. She now realises her mistake. Anthony adapted in order to survive, absorbing the dubious conventional late-Victorian creed of the public schools, and so losing his integrity. He poses as an officer and a gentleman, calling himself 'Captain Farrant' when he chooses; his flair with figures gets him jobs but he is too unreliable to keep them, and he has lied his way about the world, always 'resigning'. He is an easy fraud to recognise. The Harrow tie does not deceive Minty for two moments.

> . . . his smile explained everything; he carried it always with him as a leper carried his bell; it was a perpetual warning that he was not to be trusted. (1.1)

He is capable of precarious moments of happiness only by a complete disregard for consequences – the one guide to living he learned at school. He pursues girls, but has never grown out of his childhood devotion to his sister. He acknowledges that he has 'no future'.

Determined to make one for him and if possible to share it, Kate obtains him a job at 'Krogh's' in Stockholm where she is mistress and business assistant to the owner of this multinational company. Krogh's, which seems to manufacture everything, represents modern capitalism, more in a fable's manner than a novel's, although Greene is realistic about the glass and steel architecture of its headquarters. The narrative which shadows Krogh's worried thoughts about business sounds suitably well-informed, but the novel's objection to capitalism is simply expressed.

> The intricate network of subsidiary companies was knitted together by his personal credit. Honesty was a word which had never troubled him; a man was honest so long as his credit was good: and his credit, he could tell himself with pride, stood a point higher than the credit of the French Government. For years he had been able to borrow money at four per cent to lend to the French Government at five. That was honesty – something which could be measured in figures. (2.1)

The plot illustrates this difference between credit and honesty. Krogh's dishonesty shows when his credit is endangered at a critical stage of his expansion into America. He lies to and afterwards dismisses a union leader to avert a strike, and he falsifies documents relating to the transfer of funds intended to preserve his credit. His henchman Hall, who knew him in early days in Chicago, is a crook. He attacks with knuckledusters the sacked union leader's son, who has come to appeal for justice, and when Anthony discovers the illegalities in Krogh's papers, Hall kills him. The simple large irony, that everyone in Stockholm, including the British ambassador, admires Krogh almost to the point of worship, is mournfully emphasised throughout the book.

All the characters are, except at moments of doubtful or vicious pleasure, unhappy. Greene is not successful with them all. Krogh broods about his peasant childhood (and, even in rural Sweden, disagreeable schooling) and early successes which gave more satisfaction than his present position as 'the richest man in the world'. Greene dwells, as though from duty, on the obvious ways in which wealth and celebrity imprison him. When Anthony becomes his bodyguard, they play truant from Krogh's public responsibilities, but such enjoyments are brief and culminate in Hall's assault on the young worker. Kate is dismayed by the foolish 'innocence' of Anthony's wish to make Krogh 'human'. He must not be that if the firm is to prosper. With Anthony and Kate Greene is much more successful. They are wretched because of their incestuous love, which they do not quite recognise although their conversation sometimes flirts with the idea of it. The taboo is a 'dangerous edge'. Greene establishes the meaning of 'Kate' in Anthony's thoughts and the fact that he is unaware of it.

> But the years had trained him to be thankful for the moment, not to look forward. Now at this instant I am alone in the cubicle, now at this instant I am happy in my bunk, now for the moment only I am with Kate, with a friend. (2.3)

Repetition of the phrases which stress the momentary nature of safety and happiness, in bed in the cubicle at school or in a ship's bunk between jobs, distracts his attention from the fact that it is his sister who comes first to his mind, which then bounces away to safety in the last phrase. 'I am with Kate' is an innocent, childish thought to Anthony; Greene's mistrust of adult innocence appears in the placing of 'in my bunk'. Anthony and Kate see the 'curse' of twinhood in the loss in adult life of its special sympathies. But the sexual aspect of the frustration hovers about them. These lines occur when Kate has been showing him Krogh's headquarters.

'And through there?'
'His bedroom.'
She was ill at ease . . .

The presence of chronic unhappiness behind Anthony's thoughts
of happy moments appears in many passages. In Kate's practical
coping with dangerous business affairs and in the vulnerability
of her love for her brother, which she admits more than he can,
she is one of Greene's most interesting and intelligent female
characters. Gloom, in this relationship, is more subtle than in
It's a Battlefield. *England Made Me* has a finer pessimism than the
previous novel, although it too often protests unsubtly.

Any discussion of *England Made Me* returns to the role of
Minty. Greene's novels explore many of the ways in which a
child's troubles tug at his adult life. Anthony's thoughts in the
lines quoted are those of the schoolboy who is a genuine part of
him, still. Minty seems to have run away from Harrow and
hidden, a permanent unhappy fourteen-year-old, in his present
minimised existence. Small and feeble, a collector of butterflies
and holy pictures, he suffered so badly at school that his mother
had at last to be summoned to take him away. Apart from the
great event of his 'draining', nothing in the twenty years he has
spent in Stockholm, supplementing a small monthly remittance
by selling scraps of news to the papers, has made such an
impression on him as that of his schooldays. A group photograph
of the members of his house at school hangs over his bed. He is
a loyal Old Boy. His only prospect of conviviality is that an
Old Harrovians' dinner may be granted by the British
ambassador, Sir Ronald, usually named as 'the Minister'. (All
the male English characters are Harrovians, except Anthony
who wears the tie.) Even this is diminished because the last
dinner was a disaster; and, since his stomach was 'drained' ten
years ago, Minty has been unable to drink anything stronger
than tepid coffee. He lives in squalor and, given his income, a
poverty which Greene has, surely, exaggerated: one room, one
cup (broken), one glass. This is appropriate, however, since he
lives like a schoolboy. A complicated penknife disfigures his
pocket; Minty makes holes with this in tins of condensed milk,
which he then sucks out, as in the days of tuck-boxes. Lying,
when he promises to pay for news of Krogh obtained by
Anthony, he crosses his fingers as one did at school, to annul

the sin. The human body, male or female, disgusts him. He is yellow from nicotine. In a long overcoat, his short body is ridiculous in the streets; he knows that strangers laugh at him. His Anglo-Catholic faith is a refuge which does not protect him from paltry hatreds arising from the misery which, the text frequently insists, exudes from him. It is unsurprising, in Greene, to find such a failure thanking God in his prayers at night for 'a happy and successful day'. Minty is ridiculous even in prayer, but impressive in spite of it. Miguel de Unamuno says of Don Quixote, in *The Tragic Sense of Life*, a book Greene admired, that 'he will triumph by making himself ridiculous', and this is one way of expressing Minty's appeal.[62]

Many passages are forceful and ambivalent because as we follow Minty's thoughts we are kept uncertain whether to smile at him or to sympathise. When he shelters from the rain in the British ambassador's room, he makes his grubby poverty a weapon.

> To use powder, to take such care with one's clothes, to be so carefully brushed, the hypocrisy of it sickened Minty. The body still remained, its functions were not hidden by Savile Row. To think that God himself had become a man. Minty could not enter a church without the thought, which sickened him, which was more to him than the agony in the garden, the despair upon the Cross. Pain was an easy thing to bear beside the humiliation which rose with one in the morning and lay down with one at night. He stood and dripped at the carpet's edge and thought that at least one need not be so coarse as to love the body like Gullie or hide it under powder and pin-striped elegant suits like the Minister. Hating the hypocrites he waited for the Minister to look up, exposing his shabbiness with a mournful malicious pride. (3.3)

'He stood and dripped' sounds pathetic and aggressive at the same time. 'Mournful' is a term of approval for Greene ('in mournful happiness in the dark') and 'malicious' need not be disapproving. Minty is very far from being a saint; he is resourcefully spiteful to the Minister. But Greene is on his side against the smug diplomat who flatters Krogh in the hope of advice about his investments and says of Anthony that he must be 'straight' if he is working in Krogh's; and against the attaché

Gullie who claims, when Minty finds him perusing photographs of nudes, to have only an 'artistic' interest in them. It is a tenable view that Minty's distaste for Savile Row is connected with Greene's fondness for parts of the world too poor to disguise man's basic squalor.

Minty seems not to need the author's explicit sympathy. He makes the other characters look planned, illustrative of Greene's reproachful thoughts about human shortcomings and the sorry state of Europe, because his vitality is so unusual and impressive. It is comic, and the comedy arises from the very small scale on which he lives. Samuel Beckett's straitened people are reminiscent of Minty, and so is the brilliant comic role invented in the 1950s by Tony Hancock. A flat in Minty's building stays empty, although its rent is paid; he is 'tormented' by curiosity, but reluctant to learn about it because it is 'an interest'. He is so reduced that small perils loom large: 'although he had a new blade he did not cut himself once; he shaved cautiously rather than closely'.

> 'This is the way that Minty goes.' He picked up a stump of cigarette from the soap-tray and lit it. Then he studied his hair in the mirror of the wardrobe door; this was one of his days; he must be prepared for anything, even society. (3.1)

The last words have a hint of Proust which is nicely incongruous with the cigarette butts Minty tidily stores in his soap-dish.

His 'day', which occupies much of Part 3 and ends with the spider's revival, is a great success, on Minty's scale. He receives two letters, one his remittance, the other from 'the Family', a rare event. He outmanoeuvres the newspaper editor who tries to reprimand him, teases Anthony by chatting about Harrow (and by talking at length about the use of chasubles), and vexes the ambassador. Kate reflects on how strong weaknesses can be when she thinks about Anthony and the point is made comically in Minty's resourcefulness. He exploits the English social code: Anthony's false colours, he thinks, put him in Minty's power; the Minister has to accept him once he is into the room ('my dear fellow') and manners will not let him notice that Minty is dripping rain on the carpet, because Minty *is* a Harrovian – and therefore at ease with Sir Ronald. There is comedy in the clash between his English and Swedish roles; and his courage

in desperation makes him appealing, as a beggared gentleman.
A corresponding comedy in his talk mixes his Anglo-Catholicism
with his poverty and other humiliations.

> . . . 'almost exactly ten years ago. August the twenty-first. The
> feast-day of St Jane Frances Fremiot de Chantal, widow. I
> hung between life and death', Minty said, 'for exactly five
> days. I always put my recovery down to St Zephyrinus . . .
> they made an incision and drained me.'
>   'Drained you?'
>   'Yes, drained me. You would never believe the amount of
> pus they removed. It would have filled a milk-jug, a large
> milk-jug.' (3.2)

Explaining to Anthony that he 'keeps an eye on' Krogh, who is
always 'news', and likes to remember that Krogh is only
human, he says, 'Well, Farrant, it makes Minty feel all
evensong, all *vox humana* – "and He shall exalt the humble and
meek"'. (3.2)

Minty is not meek; he can out-talk anybody. But his 'malicious
pride' is compensated by humble aspects, such as his hopes of
friendship. Anthony accepts him as the embassy attachés do
not ('They laugh.'), and Minty counts him 'the fourth friend'.
There have been three other friendships, one very brief and
based on the gift of a bar of chocolate, at school, among fellow
outcasts. Religiously, he preserves small mementos. Mourning
Anthony at the end, he knows that 'there wouldn't be many
more'. (7) We are not invited to laugh at the friendless Minty.
His threadbare friendships, possessions ('Don't touch my
spider', he says when Anthony and a girl visit him, to use his
room [4.1].) and prayers, are real. He is comic in a way which
makes us smile at our own absurdities. At the end of the novel
we share a joke with him.

Greene complains that his character 'steals all the scenes in
which he plays a part' and has 'the last word, robbing even
Kate of her curtain at Anthony's funeral'.[63] The last word is
this.

> He put his hand in his pocket and pulled out a silver match-
> box. 'I wanted to give him this.' He twisted it to show the

engraved arms. 'I was really at Harrow, so it's no good to me. He'd have liked it.'

Kate's last word is a Socialist commonplace of the time; speaking as a business-woman, she says, 'We're all thieves'. The whole novel conveys her bitterness; Socialist readers will find that it still tells. She is unaware, which give ironic force to the idea that big business is inseparable from crime, that Anthony was murdered. The story ends tragically for her. But the novel is enriched by Minty's comic presence and his right to the last wry comment on the world's madness is thoroughly earned.

England Made Me is more experimental in style than the previous two novels. Quotations in this chapter illustrate his success with the plain, literate but 'journalistic' style of some fiction of the 1930s. Cyril Connolly's *Enemies of Promise* (1938) constructs a passage of it, which he calls the 'New Vernacular', from lines of Orwell, Isherwood and Hemingway, which would accommodate Greene – of whom Connolly's review of contemporary literature makes no mention.[64] One obvious feature is the frequency of compound sentences, often without connecting words, as in passages quoted on pp. 39, and 40. Some critics detect the influence of W. H. Auden's verse in Greene's prose.[65] There are passages in *England Made Me* which, set as verse, would pass muster in a collection of poems from Auden's period. The author of these has been reading Eliot, among other poets. Anthony is brooding.

> Many things there are to consider over thirty years,
> things seen and heard and lied about and loved,
> things one has feared and admired and felt desire for,
> things abandoned with the sea gently lifting
> and the lightship dropping behind like a small station
> on the Underground,
> bright at night and empty,
> no one getting out and the train not stopping. (1.2)

This tendency to lose his very good ear for prose rhythm, and to use sixty words to say almost nothing, soon disappeared from Greene's fiction, although Audenesque images and cadences lingered. Verse cadences occur mostly where the writer is influenced by, if not exactly practising the Joycean and Woolfean stream-of-consciousness technique, mingling nightmares, of school and clubs east of Aden, with memories of London girls, in Anthony's thoughts. Greene abandoned that too. Asked by a critic why he had done so, the novelist hero of *The End of the Affair* replies, 'Why change a flat?' (5.2).

Greene's flair for simile appears from *Stamboul Train* on. In a critical essay he attributes to François Mauriac his own 'cunning method of disguised commentary employed by Mauriac who conceals the author's voice in a simile or an unexpected adjective, like a film director who makes his personal comment with a camera angle'.[66] A nice example of an unexpected adjective is 'tired umbrella' (EMM 3.5), which catches the look of one, abandoned in a stand, and for a moment gives us an umbrella's point of view. Images in *Stamboul Train* concentrate the novel's violence and cruelty: 'her body trembled and moved under her dress like a cat tied in a bag' (3.3); 'her voice was low, almost tender; she might have been urging a loved dog towards a lethal chamber' (2.1). These 'conceal' the author's complaint at life's nastiness. Their note of amused distaste is one feature of the distinctive voice which Greene learned to give his writing. We are told that Minty is 'like a third-class berth in a boat going abroad; he seemed to have known only strangers, he carried about him the smell of oil and misery' (4.1). The leper's bell, in a simile already quoted, is a favourite of Greene's.[67] Minty's helplessness is contained in the image of the ship's berth. His stature is acknowledged elsewhere: Nils, a young Swede who tags about with Minty, 'stood at his elbow . . . with the devotion of a page in an Elizabethan play who has followed a monarch into poverty and exile' (2.3).

3

'A Catholic Novelist'

An aphorism which might stand as an epigraph to the next phase of Greene's fiction occurs at the end of *It's a Battlefield*. The prison chaplain is talking to the Assistant Commissioner.

> The chaplain said, 'I can't stand human justice any more. Its arbitrariness. Its incomprehensibility.'
> 'I don't mean, of course, to be blasphemous, but isn't that very like, that is to say, isn't divine justice much the same?'
> 'Perhaps. But one can't hand in a resignation to God.'

G. M. Young observes that 'aphorisms should be perfectly clear in form but with receding distances of meaning'.[68] The immediate background to this one is in the context. 'Perhaps' brings out the sense of wanting to resign: the believer's dissatisfaction with God's ways. Further distances of meaning occur in *Brighton Rock* (1938), *The Power and the Glory* (1940), *The Heart of the Matter* (1948) and *The End of the Affair* (1951), novels which invite the label 'Catholic novelist' because they look at the chaplain's aphorism from distinctly Catholic, although idiosyncratic, points of view.

Many modern writers who have resigned by ceasing to believe explore the 'absurdity' of a world without God. When these Greene novels contemplate the absence of God, their term is 'hell'. In an essay of 1951, Greene cited a conversation recorded by Rider Haggard, in which Kipling agreed with him that 'this world is one of the hells'.

> He replied that he did not think – he was certain of it. He went on to show that it had every attribute of hell:

doubt, fear, pain, struggle, bereavement, almost irresistible
temptations springing from the nature with which we are
clothed, physical and mental suffering, etc., ending in the
worst fate man can devise for man, Execution![69]

Greene points out that Haggard's hero Quartermain dies
reflecting that 'it is not a good world', that only the 'wilfully
blind' think it so, that 'the wonder is . . . that there should be
any good left in it', and that, after remembering the good
things, 'I should not wish to live again'. He quotes from
Haggard's novel *The Brethren* a line which *A Sort of Life*
recommends as a 'great phrase', read in childhood and never
forgotten: 'So they went, talking earnestly of all things, but,
save in God, finding no hope at all.'[70]

Greene finds Kipling's idea an intriguing heresy and although
he does not share it, he approves of its emphasis. He claims
that Dickens's novels show signs of the same 'eternal and
alluring taint', a 'simple and terrible explanation of our plight,
how the world was made by Satan and not by God, lulling us
with the music of despair'.[71] The taint is 'alluring' to Greene as
well as to Dickens because, in his view of Dickens, they share a
sense of the reality of evil. This distinguishes Greene from those
who think life ultimately absurd. It checks a character in *The
Comedians* on the verge of the absurdist belief that nothing can
be known: 'horror is aways real' (1.5.2). Evil is not the sum of
all misconduct, immorality and human error, capable of
correction, but a force which is absolute, eternal and for us
irresistible without an appeal to God. Disbelief therefore
means, to Greene, Kipling's position rather than an atheism
which also denies the devil. Christianity and other hopeful
religions are, in this view, a devilish turn of the screw, and the
devil lies to the saint or mystic. Such is not an easy belief to live
with; it is not far from Greene's doubtful Catholicism, which
believes in God as a desperate last resort. This makes our
world 'one of the hells', a region (or regions) from which
escape is possible, although difficult. It is peopled by damned
souls, however, who have little evident hope of redemption, and
by would-be escapers who are in constant danger of recapture.
They live 'on the dangerous edge of things', and Greene's most
obviously religious novels are melodramas set on the edge of
hellish regions of innocents who cannot see the dangers.

. . . the greatness and littleness of man, his far-reaching aims, his short duration, the curtain hung over his futurity, the disappointments of life, the defeat of good, the success of evil, physical pain, mental anguish, the prevalence and intensity of sin, the pervading idolatries, the corruptions, the dreary hopeless irreligion, that condition of the whole race, so fearfully yet exactly described in the Apostle's words, 'having no hope and without God in the world' – all this is a vision to dizzy and appal; and inflicts upon the mind the sense of a profound mystery, which is absolutely beyond human solution.

What shall be said to this heart-piercing, reason-bewildering fact? I can only answer, that either there is no Creator, or this living society of men is in a true sense discarded from His presence . . . *if* there be a God, since there is a God, the human race is implicated in some terrible aboriginal calamity.[72]

Greene set this quotation at the front of *The Lawless Roads* (1939), together with the first half, omitted here, of the great sentence in which Cardinal Newman summarises life. In *Brighton Rock* various characters come to a different view: 'it's a good life'; 'the world's all right'. Greene wrote four 'religious' novels to dizzy and appal their complacency. They appal by insisting upon the calamitous nature of life, but they can dizzy, too, at best, in their peculiar sense of comedy.

Brighton Rock's first sentence announces a thriller: 'Hale knew, before he had been in Brighton three hours, that they meant to murder him.' The opening scenes show the circumstances in which Pinkie murders him and the waitress Rose witnesses a clue as skilfully as in any thriller. But we soon see that the novel will go beyond the limits of an adventure story. Its villain Pinkie is a young psychopath; he sees himself as a damned soul. The detective-story's role of the just citizen who pursues a criminal when the police will not belongs to Ida Arnold, an 'immense' woman, big-breasted (as the text constantly reminds us) and big-hearted. She gathers her evidence and is in at the kill, but Pinkie destroys himself and, where the normal thriller justifies its violent excitements by asserting that right wins the game, *Brighton Rock* asserts that human justice is inadequate and irrelevant to the real struggle against evil.

One of the novel's strengths is that it makes violence horrible. Pinkie learned sadism at school where he tortured 'soft boys' in the playground with the sharp 'dividers' issued for geometry – Greene supposing a Board School to be basically as rich a breeding-ground for evil as Berkhamsted. Now seventeen, he has advanced to the razor-blade, the weapon of the protection-racketeers who operated at Brighton racecourse in the 1930s. The leader of his gang has been razored to death by a rival's men and he is in charge. The physical nastiness of this type of fighting is very well conveyed in the scene where Pinkie is attacked at the race track.

> The mob were enjoying themselves, just as he had always enjoyed himself. One of them leant forward to cut his cheek, and when he put up his hand to shield himself they slashed his knuckles again. He began to weep, as the four-thirty went by in a drum-beat of hooves. (4.1)

This needs no adjective. The pain races in the hooves. Discussing his difficulty in learning to present action, Greene refers to his model, R. L. Stevenson, and quotes: 'It came all of a sudden when it did, with a rush of feet and a roar and then a shout from Alan and the sound of blows and someone crying as if hurt. I looked back over my shoulder and saw Mr Shuan in the doorway crossing blades with Alan.' He comments, 'not even an adjective'.[73] But if Greene learned the swiftness and immediacy of action from Stevenson, he uses it differently. The crossing of blades in the lines from *Kidnapped* is thrilling. The mob's enjoyment is made unpleasant by the sense of being a helpless victim, to be cut here or there.

Pleasure in violence and cruelty always appears, in *Brighton Rock*, in relation to the horrors of the playground; it is an infantile lust. At the prospect of watching his henchman Spicer 'carved' to death, Pinkie enjoys 'the finest of all sensations, the infliction of pain'.

> He turned on Spicer with secret venom, cruelty straightening his body like lust.
> 'Yes', he said, putting his arm round Spicer's shoulder. (4.1)

The gesture of friendship which hides intentions looks like a child's because there are so many allusions to playground tortures and because there is so much emphasis on Pinkie's youth. he is 'the Boy'. He drinks squashes while the gang have whisky; he does not smoke or bet; he has never kissed a girl, their lips revolt him. The most vicious amusements of childhood have trapped him in perversion. When, just before his death, he meets a youth he knew at school and says with relish, 'I used to give him hell in the breaks' (7.7), the commonplace 'give him hell' has a peculiar resonance. The misery of childhood is part of it. When he dies, his face is 'like a child's, badgered, confused, betrayed: fake years slipped away – he was whisked back towards the unhappy playground' (7.10). Pinkie is a fully developed sadist, but is only unnatural in degree; the mob, naturally, enjoy carving. In the backstreets of Brighton are shops which sell under-the-counter magazines. 'Spicer used to get them. About girls being beaten. Full of shame to expose herself thus before the boys she stooped . . .' (6.2). The romantic stories on the counter, Pinkie says in effect when these are mentioned, are a false cover. Devilry, *Brighton Rock* urges, is human nature, though concealed in the innocent-looking crowds at the sea-side.

Pinkie's devilry is open and acknowledged, and the novel urges that, given the desperate human predicament, this is his only hope. He is a believing Catholic; if he can achieve remorse, the confessional will give him absolution. He is obsessed by the tag, 'Between the stirrup and the ground, He mercy sought and mercy found', but he learns under the mob's razors that last-minute remorse is very difficult for one lacking the regular discipline of confession. The plot traces the stages of his descent to damnation, with the classical idea of 'easy to fall' always present: the way up is harder; evil drags one down. Greene touches his character with his own fascination at the lengths to which evil can go, and with something of his horror, until he tempts Rose to suicide and so to her damnation. At the moments when Pinkie remembers from church-days, *'dona nobis pacem'*, yearning for God's peace, and the possibility that he might turn to it flickers, Greene is equal to Bernanos in his power to stir interest, even in readers who do not believe in the peace of God when they set the book down.

The novel invites comparison with Elizabethan tragedy when
Pinkie's crooked lawyer quotes 'This is hell nor are we out of
it', from Marlowe's tragic devil Mephistopheles in *Doctor Faustus*.
With Shakespeare's tragedies in mind, Greene stresses the force
of events which make it impossible for Pinkie to go back once
the killing has started, or to make himself safe by killing. Rose's
knowledge of Spicer's involvement in the murder of Hale means
that to be safe Pinkie must kill Spicer. Then he decides that
Rose's knowledge will never let him feel safe and he plans her
death. He cries in desperation just before he dies, asking
whether he must have 'a massacre' to be safe. But if this aspect
of the story puts the death of Macbeth in mind, Pinkie is like
Richard III in a fascination with how evil he can be. His
secular marriage means that he and Rose will live in mortal sin,
unable to confess, to be damned if they die impenitent. At his
wedding Pinkie feels 'awe' at his power to destroy a soul.
Finally he tempts her to kill herself, pretending that he means
to do the same. Of course the novel suffers, like most literature,
in comparison with Shakespeare and Marlowe. Greene attends
so much less to 'the greatness of man' in Newman's phrase
than to 'the littleness'. Faustus is tragic because his poetry
makes him great – 'See how Christ's blood streams in the
firmament'. Greene's story arouses terror and pity on its far
smaller scale.

Like Shakespearean tragedy, the novel draws attention to the
cruelty of laughter. The gangsters laugh like Elizabethans at
cruelty and abuse. Rose laughs at a photograph of Spicer
looking frightened to death (3.3). One of Greene's best short
stories, 'The Destructors', ends with the collapse of an old
man's house, engineered by a gang of small boys, and an
onlooker laughs. The owner asks 'how dare you laugh?' and is
told 'I can't help it . . . you got to admit it's funny.' An
educated sense of humour includes a graduated awareness of
what is not amusing, but also a memory of primitive laughter.
Some of the nastiest scenes in *Brighton Rock* contain glimpses of
how they might have been made to look funny, as when Pinkie
threatens Rose with vitriol on his first date, because it is more
effective with 'polonies' than a knife. The novel ends with two
of Greene's most memorable Satanic jokes. Pinkie has been
obsessed with the frail hope of death's door repentance. He dies
when his bottle of vitriol, struck by a policeman's truncheon,

explodes in his face, sending him reeling over a cliff in too great an agony to think. A priest consoles Rose in the confessional; there may be hope, given God's illimitable mercy, granted that he loved her – as she believes. She hopes that she is carrying his baby and she goes home comforted by remembering that Pinkie recorded a message for her on their wedding-night, which she has never heard. This will be a loved voice from the dead. We know that her vulcanite disc will say, 'God damn you, you little bitch, why can't you go back home for ever, and let me be?' The word 'home' has the most unhappy connotations for Rose; she loved Pinkie because he rescued her from there. In such ironies Greene dares us to laugh.

The novel appals and dizzies. The dizziness unsettles us by hovering on the edge of comedy.

'Stop a moment. Stop a moment,' the man said. 'You be quiet, mother.' He said to the Boy, 'We couldn't let Rose go not for ten nicker – not to a stranger. How do we know you'd treat her right?'

'I'll give you twelve,' the Boy said. 'It's not a question of money,' the man said. 'I like the look of you. We wouldn't want to stand in the way of Rose bettering herself – but you're too young.'

'Fifteen's my limit,' the Boy said. 'Take it or leave it.'

'You can't do anything without we say yes,' the man said. The Boy moved a little away from Rose. 'I'm not all that keen.'

'Make it guineas.' (5.3)

To marry Rose Pinkie needs her parents' permission, even though the lawyer Mr Prewitt can manage things, because she is only sixteen. 'I like the look of you' reminds us of Pinkie's pink skin and nasty eyes: the text calls them 'grey, inhuman . . . eyes' (1.1) and 'ageless': 'when you met him face to face he looked older, the slatey eyes were touched with the annihilating eternity from which he had come and to which he went' (1.2). Victorian melodrama could not make eyes sound more sinister. More convincing is the look which silences Spicer (4.1) and the single word 'purpose' which tells us of the murder. The novel shows no sense of what would have amused Max Beerbohm, and pleased his character Enoch Soames, in the portentous rhythm and diction of the sentence about 'annihilating eternity'. But Pinkie is a potentially comic figure. *Doctor Faustus* and much medieval literature and art which represents the devil and his works allows for the grotesquely comic aspect of evil; when this awareness is lacking, as in the worst 'decadent' writing of the 1890s, there is a temptation to laugh at the representation, as Beerbohm laughs at the decadents in his story, 'Enoch Soames'. 'I like the look of you' puts Pinkie in a necessary comic perspective.

If we think of the scene of very light comedy, in Shaw's *Pygmalion*, where Mr Doolittle tries to haggle with Professor Higgins over a price for his daughter, the contrast shows the darkness of Greene's humour and the strength of his irony. Both scenes rely on the traditional, middle-class amusement at the frankness and small scale of financial arrangements in lower-class marriages: 'We couldn't let Rose go not for ten nicker', 'Make it guineas', 'Not to a stranger' and 'How do we know you'd treat her right?' These lines combine with 'I like the look of you' and 'you're too young', to concentrate the irony of all the father does not know about the abnormality of Pinkie's suit.

Brighton Rock does not let us take refuge in its moments of comedy. They are subdued by the cruelty of the situations in which they occur, and by the language, which makes a cacophany of words which express extreme distaste: 'nausea', 'poison', 'venom', 'disgust', 'horror', 'humiliation', 'repulsion', 'hideous', 'stale', 'grim', 'sour', 'awful'. Derogatory adjectives are very conspicuous. The slum where Rose lives is, within the few pages of 5.3, 'awful', 'dingy' (twice), 'damaged', 'dreary', 'shabby', 'deformed', 'dusty', 'dreadful', 'battered', 'hopeless', 'horrifying', 'evil', and full of 'lavatory' smells. Intensifying adjectives are another feature of the writing. In one section (6.2), Pinkie suffers 'an enormous pressure of pride'; he has 'an enormous urge to confession'; the registrar at his wedding gives him (understandably) 'a glance of intense dislike'; he feels 'an immeasurable victory'; Rose speaks with 'immense relief'. Elsewhere another character feels 'an enormous depression' and then 'a sense of the immeasurable sadness of injustice' (6.1); Pinkie is 'conscious of his enormous ambitions' (5.1); Ida has 'an enormous sense of well-being' and smiles 'with enormous and remote tenderness' (7.6).

An obvious objection to the flood of adjectives is that they say so little. A novelist who had never seen a slum could safely use all Greene's terms for the back streets of Brighton; they would equally well apply to an African shanty town. Sometimes a sentence is shaped so that every word must tell: 'with immense labour and immense patience they extricated from the long day the grain of pleasure' (1.1). 'Immense' is needed here for balance of rhythm and ironic effect, preparing for 'grain'. But 'immense' and kindred words occur so often that, rereading the novel, we may feel that the tiresome efforts involved in a day at the seaside are not strictly 'immense', and so lose sympathy with Greene's loathing of all such superficial enjoyments, because he has devalued the word. Adjectives sometimes attach to nouns too precise to be modified: 'immense glee' occurs once. Glee is glee.

As in Conrad and D. H. Lawrence, it is hard to decide whether the emphasis works. It can be read as a violence in the writing, an impatience with the good taste which expects adjectives to be minimised and chosen with care; they show the strength of feeling of a writer who is a craftsman with words but, given the poverty and violence of Brighton's low life, at a loss for them. One might argue that the words which describe Rose's slum belong to Pinkie, reflecting the poverty and nagging unease of his mind. But they do not all belong to his diction. He would use another word for 'lavatory', and his most frequent adjectives would be poorer than Greene's.

It is true that even George Orwell is never more firm about the wretchedness of the English poor of the 1930s than Greene is here, and in *It's a Battlefield*. But Greene is at his most fiercely Catholic in this novel. Poverty is not the problem. Rose's slum contains 'murder, copulation [a conjunction typical of *Brighton Rock*], extreme poverty, fidelity and the love and fear of God' (4.2). In some of Pinkie's thoughts about marriage, the idiosyncratic nature of Greene's Catholicism creates a typical grim paradox: 'she was good, he'd discovered that, and he was damned: they were made for each other' (4.3). This particular jest gives way to the novel's most serious theme, which the narrative commentary and the characters frequently explain to us: human judgement about right and wrong is futile because it has no bearing on the conflict of good and evil. Pinkie embodies evil, and Rose goodness; human judgement takes the plump

form of Ida Arnold, who strives to bring Pinkie to justice and to
rescue Rose. In the ungloomy fictional world of Mr Savory, she
would be a heroine; her life is a great gay round, loving a
laugh, a drink, a chat, a superstitious thrill at the ouija board, a
man for the afternoon, a flutter at the races. She is not religious,
but she knows what is right. In her sense of British justice, as
well as in her cheery hedonism, she is meant to represent
English paganism, and so she does. Greene hates it, and his
narrative commentary condemns it.

> she was honest, she was kindly, she belonged to the great
> middle law-abiding class, her amusements were their
> amusements, her superstitions their superstitions . . . she had
> no more love for anyone than they had. (3.1)

Rose is even more severe: 'I'd rather burn like you', she tells
Pinkie, 'than be like Her . . . She's ignorant' (4.1).
   The novel alienates Ida from its real world where good and
evil conflict, amidst poverty. The last paragraph of the scene
where Rose is sold for fifteen guineas dwells on the 'lavatory
smells' in her house (5.3); the next section begins, 'Ida Arnold
bit an éclair and the cream spurted between the large front
teeth'. Greene presents Ida as a fleshy figure (never forgetting
her big breasts) and comments by stressing disagreeable aspects
of the human body – pimples, bad teeth, abscesses, stomach
pains, nausea and ugliness. The portrayal of Brighton is
'unrealistic' in the sense that it does not allow us to see the
town Ida would see. The details selected show only dirt,
deformity, vulgarity: a child in the street has an iron brace on
its leg (5.3); the walls of the registry office look like a public
lavatory (6.2). This is the Brighton a devil might see, or a
Jonathan Swift. Greene's point is that since the devil exists, Ida
Arnold cannot see the real Brighton, poised on the brink of hell.
Life, Ida thinks, is 'sunlight on brass bedposts, Ruby port'
(1.3). The narrative mocks her, with dark amusement, on the
same page, when smoke rises from a crematorium: 'it had been
a busy day at the furnaces'.
   The half-smile in that sentence is typical of the book. Pinkie's
absurdity as a boy in charge of gangsters – newspapers confirm
from time to time that this happens — is sometimes allowed to
be just amusing:

'Yes,' the Boy said, 'we'll have some ice-cream.'

'Stow it, Pinkie,' Dallow protested when the girl had left them, 'we don't want ice-cream. We ain't a lot of tarts, Pinkie.' (1.2)

although the innocent note in his preference clashes with the fact that he has just committed murder. The others are off their food. A similar droll touch makes him secure his false alibi in an amusement arcade. There is a persistent quiet comedy of language when the mob's peculiar standards make ordinary speech sound odd. 'I was always against murder,' Spicer said. 'I don't care who knows it' (2.1). In the first section of Part Six, one of Pinkie's men, disaffected, goes out into Brighton and the narrative follows his thoughts. He buys a printed love letter, addressed from 'Cupid's Wings, Amor Lane' and worded in appropriate diction: 'you have crushed the very soul out of me, as the butterfly on the wheel . . .'

Cubitt grinned uneasily. He was deeply moved. That was what always happened to you if you took up with anything but a buer; they gave you the air. Grand Renunciations, Tragedies, Beauty moved in Cubitt's brain. If it was a buer of course you took a razor to her, carved her face, but this love printed here was class. He read on: it was literature.

This passage creates an intriguing context for the words 'deeply', 'of course', and the capitalised grandeur. When Cubitt applies for a job with a much greater and more respectable gang leader, Colleoni, a few pages later, and a henchman explains that Mr Colleoni may be going into politics – 'the Conservatives think a lot of him' – the irony is lost on them, although we remember that Mr Colleoni liked the new look of Pinkie when they met, and offered him a place in one of his gangs. 'Think a lot of him' is bizarre in this setting, amusingly casual. When Cubitt meets Ida (a necessary plot-device since she learns from him that Hale was murdered), he feels that there are times 'when a man needed a woman's understanding', and he confesses that he has 'never held' with murder. 'Carving's different', he says. 'Of course, carving's different', Ida agrees, soothingly, in her role as mum to all the world. 'Carving' is a word which grows familiar in the course of the novel and joins the many gruesome half-jokes with which

Greene tempts the reader into sharing the novel's point of view.

Pinkie's name is almost a joke, part of a small comedy of names. Greene likes colour-names. Pinkie's surname is Brown. Rose (like Coral) is a favourite Greene name for girls. Pinkie and Rose are ludicrously matched by their names, although nobody notices. (Pinkie has no sense of humour and finds smiling physically difficult.) A much discussed racehorse, which wins Ida enough money to continue her hunt, is Black Boy. Pink Boy is a loser. The text points out that Ida's name is appropriately pagan (1.1), ancient Greek in origin but vulgar in England. Like Pinkie, the gangsters have odd non-Christian names. The lawyer is Mr Prewitt; he has come down in the world and his name sounds aptly genteel. He is a remarkably successful figure of fun, hunting in a soap-dish for his fee of one pound when Pinkie murders Spicer, or confessing his secret lust for the 'little typists' who 'go by carrying their cases' a phrase which Greene claims echoes Beatrix Potter. Prewitt is a public-school man who thinks ill of Harrow – 'a rotten set they were. No *esprit de corps*' (7.3). Such remarks are lost on Pinkie, who, like Cubitt, is comic and pathetic in the narrowness of his culture; asked what 'Memento Mori' means, he answers, 'It's foreign'. We are not often to laugh, reading *Brighton Rock*, but Greene has engrained it with his unlaughing sense of humour, which records the dizzying nature of the world.

The Power and the Glory began as a comic anecdote which Greene heard when he travelled in Mexico to report President Calles's revolutionary persecution of the Catholic Church, in 1938. A 'whisky-priest' in Chiapas had, when drunk, insisted on baptising a boy 'Brigitta'.[74] Greene turned this small joke into a legend. Much of the novel shows what is not funny about being a sinful priest in desperate circumstances. But it has its own sense of humour, and the clue to the priest's endurance is his frightened giggle. He knows that 'you only had to turn up the underside of any situation and out came scuttling these small absurd contradictory situations' (2.1). *The Power and the Glory* swarms with them.

The title of its fourth chapter, 'The Bystanders', might stand for the whole of Part One. It introduces a variety of indifferent, complacent, innocent characters, Mexican and English. We first see the priest in the company of Mr Tench, an English dentist trapped in Mexico by the fall of the peso. When the priest (who is nameless throughout) says of happier past times, 'They had at any rate – God', he replies, 'There's no difference in the teeth'. It is the dentist not the priest who is preposterous, as they chat over brandy; the body not the soul. Dentistry is absurd to Greene: a cast found in a waste-paper basket was the child Tench's favourite toy, and although his parents 'tempted him with meccano', he had found his vocation. The Chief of Police is corrupt in body and soul; he suffers chronic toothache. The priest, in flight from him, hides in the home of an English family called Fellows. Tench is unhappy but only because he is unsuccessful. Ominously, the first paragraph of Chapter 3 announces, of Captain Fellows: 'He was a happy man'. Unsurprisingly, he is a smug and shallow fake-innocent, 'borne up on a big tide of boyish joy – doing a man's job, the heart of the wild'; he likes the wild because he can feel superior to it; a good Englishman, he condemns the priest at once when asked for brandy – 'What a religion!' The novel firmly connects the consolations of alcohol and religion – symbolised by sacramental wine; those who need neither or try to suppress both have cut themselves off from suffering. Mrs Fellows is paralysed by a faithless fear of death. Their enterprising thirteen-year-old daughter, Coral, runs the plantation and shelters the priest, giving him beer and advice, although, tutored by a London correspondence course, she lost her Protestant faith when she was ten.

Conspicuous among the Mexican bystanders is Padre José who has obeyed the new law that priests must renounce their faith and marry. His wife nags him, and the children mock him in the street. The mother of a Mexican family, whose young son Luis is to be a key figure at the end, is a complacent Catholic quick to condemn José and to disapprove of Luis's talking to him. José's extreme failure and suffering, in estrangement from his faith, are shown with sympathy and with characteristic interest in 'positive' temptation in the sense in which Rose, in *Brighton Rock*, is 'tempted' not to kill herself: 'An enormous temptation came to Padre José to take the risk and say a prayer' (1.4). José is in no position to be complacent and, though steeped in sin and despair, he seems superior to those who are. The virtuous police lieutenant who is the priest's principal antagonist is a contrived figure. Greene says that he had to invent him because there were no virtuous police officers in Mexico; the other characters were suggested by people he met. The lieutenant is invented rather than imagined. He is a believer in the revolution, dignified by his 'idea' of destroying superstition and poverty. He blames the Church for these and for the misery of his childhood and he tells himself that he acts on behalf of the children who will grow up in a better, Godless Mexico. His hatred of 'ease, safety, toleration and complacency', represented by the Fellows family, recommends him to the novel's judgement, but a smile is permitted behind his back. He watches the children playing an 'obscure' game in the plaza, not knowing what we have learned from Luis, that the heroes of their games are the priests he has shot.

> We all of us play them. Yesterday I was Madero. They shot me in the plaza – the law of flight . . . We tossed up. I was Madero: Pedro had to be Huerta. He fled to Vera Cruz down by the river. Manuel chased him . . . (1.4)

Meanwhile, upcountry, the last priest hears confessions in a village, while a boy keeps lookout.

The last words of Chapter 3, 'the boy who watched the ford for soldiers', have the ring of an adventure story, and Greene, like Luis, obviously approves of priests as wanted men: the whisky-priest's photograph appears on a 'wanted' poster beside that of a gangster, and the lieutenant asserts that he is much the more 'dangerous'. The romantic appeal is, none the less, restrained. The tone of the narrative, in Part 1, is more often one of wry amusement touched by dismay. The famous vultures of the first paragraph watch the human scene with 'shabby indifference'; Mr Tench 'wasn't carrion yet'. There is no sign of the ether cylinder he has been waiting for, but 'a little additional pain was hardly noticeable in the huge abandonment' (1.1). José 'stood outside himself and wondered if he was even fit for hell', but Luis says, 'He told me he was more of a martyr than the rest' (1.2). Since it is now a crime to own a religious picture or any alcoholic drink stronger than the expensive State beer, almost everyone is a criminal, and words change connotations, oddly.

> 'He is wanted on a very serious charge.'

'Murder?'

'No. Treason.'

'Oh, treason,' Captain Fellows said, all his interest dropping; there was so much treason everywhere – it was like petty larceny in a barracks. (1.3)

'Priest' now denotes 'criminal' and that, like the indifference to treason, is quietly relished throughout. When Coral takes charge of the priest, her father objects that as foreigners they should not interfere with politics. She answers, 'This isn't politics. I know about politics. Mother and I are doing the Reform Bill' (1.3). The distance between education in England and reality in other parts of the contemporary world amuses Greene here, and later, when the priest looks at Coral's schoolbooks and disapproves of Tennyson's 'The Brook' – 'the triteness and untruth of "for ever" shocked him a little; a poem like this ought not to be in a child's hands' (2.4). Sometimes a faintly amused simile contains a comment. The priest arrives in a village with only the uppers of his shoes intact, carrying his attaché case 'as if he were a season-ticket holder' (1.3). The image expresses the author's disapproval of these emblems of a former respectability. The priest is not allowed to keep the case for long.

The devil hunts down Pinkie; God, as well as the lieutenant, hunts and catches the whisky-priest. Pinkie believes himself to be damned; the priest fears that he may be damned, but preaches to the villagers that 'heaven is here' because they prepare for it in suffering. This conventional thought is part of his presentation. He used to be a fat, complacent, successful man, before the troubles. Hardships, though, have broken his discipline. He needs alcohol; while drunk, he has fathered a child, and since he loves the little Brigitta – a girl, who is shown as unlovable to an exaggerated extent – he cannot properly repent of that sin. Further humiliation arises early in Part 2, when he learns that the lieutenant is taking hostages and shooting them if their villages harbour him. His 'woman' tells him that the Church will be mocked if he becomes a martyr; if he does not, he will make martyrs. But it is his duty to remain free, to hear confessions and celebrate Mass. His predicament is 'appalling' – a word Greene frequently employs. 'He couldn't even say Mass any longer – he had no wine. It

had all gone down the dry gullet of the Chief of Police. It was –
appallingly – complicated' (2.3).

It is more so than he is aware. The thought comes when the
hero is in prison for possession of brandy, following one of the
best scenes in the novel, where he buys a bottle of wine on the
black market only to see it misappropriated by the secular arm.
Prohibition, like censorship, is comical in various ways: one
arises from *quis custodiet?* – the police become the people most
likely to drink. A beggar leads the priest, now dressed as a
peasant, to a cousin of the Governor who gets supplies from the
Customs, and advises offering this 'very important man' a glass
of brandy (2.2). The Governor's cousin prefers wine; and so
does the jefe, or Chief of Police, who soon joins them. While
breaking one law by drinking, he unknowingly enforces another
by ensuring that none of the wine can be illegally
transubstantiated. The priest weeps and has to explain away
his tears as the result of the brandy he is drinking: 'it always
takes me like this'.

> 'Forgive me, gentlemen. I get very drunk very easily and then
> I see . . .'
> 'See what?'
> 'Oh, I don't know, all the hope of the world draining away.'
> 'Man, you're a poet.' (2.2)

Because the priest means the words literally, not poetically, all
the hope of the world, in his sense, is draining away down the
Police Chief's gullet. 'Man, you're a poet' alludes to the fact
that he speaks as a priest. Comedy of this kind is reminiscent of
medieval religious drama.

Devils and other enemies of God in those plays are comic
because they cannot win and do not know it. In suppressing
religion, the Chief of Police acts, in the novel's Catholic view,
as God's adversary, and he (although not often the lieutenant)
is appropriately a figure of fun in this and other scenes. The
novel deals with a very paradoxical situation. Religious
persecution in a devout country is a sorry affair; but granted
the novel's assumption that God exists, it is completely
ridiculous to make him illegal. However appalling the condition
of the Church in this region of Mexico, it cannot be defeated.
The absurdity of the attempt appears in the comic spectacle of

the jefe drinking God's wine. The priest weeps because he is the servant of God, but such a servant cannot lose. His words, fittingly, laugh at his predicament while he weeps for it. There are other, subsurface jokes, some wildly grotesque. The lapsed Catholics ridicule themselves in drunken religious speculation. The jefe says that his earliest memory is his first communion, which reflects nicely on the use he makes today of communion wine: 'Ah, the thrill of my soul'.

> 'No, but as I was saying – life has such ironies. It was my painful duty to watch the priest who gave me that communion shot – an old man. I am not ashamed to say that I wept. The comfort is that he is probably a saint and that he prayed for us. It is not everyone who earns a saint's prayers.'
> 'An unusual way . . .'
> 'But then life is mysterious.'
> '*Salud!*' (2.2)

This passage simultaneously recalls the danger of the priest's present company and, in all the ironies which the jefe does not see, makes him look almost too much a buffoon to be dangerous. The fact that the priest can weep while listening to so farcical a speech stresses how intent he is on the wine. This scene shows in little the paradoxes which the novel expresses in its interplay of tragic and comic modes.

Like a hero in tragedy, the priest is gradually stripped of the costume and all the insignia of his rank. He has lost his altar-stone. He loses his breviary in the first chapter. The soles of his shoes (signs of rank in Mexico) wear out; the uppers and the rest of his clerical costume go next. He abandons his last priestly possession, an old scrap of paper with notes for an address to his parishioners, when he is about to be arrested for the brandy. His thoughts strip him of pride, and of ignorance of the appalling nature of the world, as he moves among the poor, and, like them, learns what prison is like. 'Outside among the hammocks the sergeant began to laugh. "Hombre", he said, "hombre, have you never been in jail before?"' (2.2). Most open laughter in the novel is cruel.

The 'Judas' figure of the half-caste police informer, seeking the price on the priest's head, adds to his sufferings by complaining, whenever they are together, of the priest's 'unjust suspicions'. In the humility which suffering teaches, the priest thinks himself no better than even this meanest wretch. He does not argue with the Protestant couple who house him when he has reached the relative safety of the next Mexican province, meekly answering the anti-Catholic jibes of the German American, Mr Lehr. When the half-caste has lured him back across the border to attend to the dying American gunman (a Catholic) whose picture has been displayed with his own on 'wanted'-boards, the lieutenant is waiting for him. In the last pages of Part 3, riding Christ-like on a mule, he reaches an ultimate humility, believing that he has failed in everything.

He does not fail to keep a sense of humour which is minimised but not quite extinguished until the very end. The priest giggles. Early on, he remembers his former ambitions to rise in the priesthood 'as something vaguely comic', and 'he gave a little gulp of astonished laughter' (2.1). In the same spirit he giggles when his Judas says he would be good if he were rich, because he remembers the children of Mary eating pastries. He giggles again soon afterwards when he reflects that the reward-money for his capture will give the Judas a year's security, which may be enough to save his soul: 'he could never take the complications of destiny quite seriously' (2.2). He giggles when the beggar asks him if he hasn't a heart (2.2). In prison, feeling relaxed, as 'one criminal among a herd of criminals', he is amused while talking to a pious woman.

> 'I had good books in my house,' she announced, with unbearable pride. He had done nothing to shake her complacency. He said, 'They are everywhere. It's no different here.'
> 'Good books?'
> He giggled. 'No, no. Thieves, murderers . . .' (2.3)

The priest tries to shake the woman's complacency by insisting on his own sins: 'He said sternly, "Oh, I am not only a drunkard"' (2.3). The incongruity of the stern rebuke and the confession is of a kind he recognises at less serious moments. By the time he is captured, his giggles have grown feebler. He giggles 'unconvincingly' when arguing about miracles with the lieutenant. When the lieutenant reports that Padre José will not come to give him absolution, on the night before his execution, only because his wife will not let him, he sees the joke although too frightened now to laugh. '"Poor man". He tried to giggle but no sound could have been more miserable than the half-hearted attempt' (3.4). He has already confessed, in a manner, to the lieutenant but has not noticed the irony there. The feeling that events have exhausted laughter, on this final day, appears too in the lieutenant, who has been depressed by finding his prisoner likeable. Luis calls to him and 'he tried to smile back, an odd sour grimace without triumph or hope. One had to begin again with that' (3.4).

There is no attempt to conceal the contrivance of the ending. We learn that the girl has died in a scene which explains how the priest has dreamed of her, serving him with wine. His dream of heaven contrasts with the lieutenant's nightmare of hell: 'laughter, laughter all the time and a long passage in which he could find no door' (3.4). We watch the execution through the eyes of Mr Tench who has left the jefe with his tooth drilled out, in the dentist's chair; we are meant to remember from the prison scene the remark that toothache is worse than the pain of the bullets which lasts a split second. The priest shares a joke, after death, with Luis. His mother has reached the end of a story she has been reading aloud in the evenings. The life of a martyred priest is told in the simplistic, idealising terms of cheap Catholic writing for the young. Luis finds it foolish and boring, except for the shooting. As he thinks of the death of the whisky-priest, who once stayed at the house, he regrets that there are now no priests left, no heroes; and now he spits when he sees the lieutenant, to whom he used to be devoted. Next night he dreams that the priest is laid out for burial while he sits by and his mother reads a pious tale about the new martyr.

> He was very bored and very tired. . . . Suddenly the dead priest winked at him – an unmistakable flicker of the eyelid, just like that.
>   He woke and there was the crack, crack on the knocker on the outer door. (4)

The priest giggled in prison when the pious woman called him a martyr. His wink is appropriate as a shared comment on the mother's story. It is also a hint. At the door is a stranger, who has just come up the river: 'My name is Father . . .'. The boy kisses the new priest's hand 'before the other could give himself a name' in the last words where the Church triumphs. The nameless whisky-priest is remembered a few lines earlier; the stranger has 'a rather sour mouth', but also 'a frightened smile'. Where 'laughter, laughter all the time', in the lieutenant's nightmare or the street urchins' mockery of Padre José, is abominable, a frightened smile in a sour mouth makes an apt image for the positive role of comedy in an appalling, dizzying world.

The Power and the Glory was the last of Greene's pre-war novels. These include two thrillers, *A Gun for Sale* (1936) and *The Confidential Agent* (1939), discussed with other entertainments and novellas, in Chapter 5. However the scale of his success is judged, there is no doubt that he had already made a name in the sense that 'Graham Greene' was, by 1942, as evocative as 'Evelyn Waugh', for those who knew the books. (Widespread fame came later.) Like Waugh, he had made his kind of novel into a genre. One of its features is a willingness to take risks. *Stamboul Train* and *England Made Me* use settings unknown or little known to the author and he had spent only a few weeks in Mexico. Foreign backgrounds were more of a risk because the novels set in England show the manners, talk and culture of the 1930s – songs, advertisements, anecdotes, headlines and slang – persuasively and with a greater social breadth than most British novelists attempted.

They take risks too with style. There is a boldness which is, when successful, one of the best features of Greene's writing: 'he drank the brandy down like damnation' (*PG* 3.1) has a Metaphysical wit, but 'he flickered like an early movie' (*BR* 6.1) is off-day Wodehouse. *Brighton Rock* has better images. Colleoni's eyes 'gleamed like raisins' (2.1); the girls in the grand hotel are 'small tinted creatures, who rang like expensive glass when they were touched' (2.1); 'goal-keepers padded like armadilloes' is one of several fresh, happy images in the second paragraph of the first chapter of Part Four. 'The sea stretched like a piece of gay common washing in a tenement square across the end of the street', is too second-hand to belittle the sea. A woman's legs – 'dead white . . . like something which has lived underground' (7.1) – is better. But 'the [dead] child lay under the streaming rain like a dark heap of cattle dung'

(*PG* 2.4) is undergraduate, not the work of the artist of unpleasantness that Greene is; disgust is not earned by the newness or exactness of the image.

He took another risk with adjectives and adverbs in *Brighton Rock* and in *The Power and the Glory* where they convey horror and degrees of that and other feelings more than they need: 'he had an immense self-importance' (*PG* 2.1); 'with a look of immense responsibility' (1.3); 'the child . . . stood . . . looking in with infinite patience.' Sometimes an abstract noun needs intensifying: 'An enormous temptation came to Padre José to say a prayer' (1.4). 'Enormous' is right because God is the tempter. After the dream on his last night, the priest wakes up 'with a huge feeling of hope' (3.4). The hope is of heaven, but 'huge' like 'enormous' would count more if Greene did not enlarge so many feelings in this novel. The dubious word 'awful' is used very often.

A different sort of risk extends the author's omniscience, in both novels, into the supernatural. God or his angel comes hunting for Pinkie's repentance, at the end of his life.

> An enormous emotion beat on him; it was like something trying to get in; the pressure of gigantic wings against the glass. Dona nobis pacem . . . If the glass broke, if the beast – whatever it was – got in, God knows what it would do. He had a sense of huge havoc – the confession, the penance and the sacrament – and awful distraction, and he drove blind into the rain. (*BR* 7.9)

This would be better with fewer adjectives. It is good that we think at first that the wings are the devil's; they are more acceptable, in Pinkie's tormented mind, than they would be in the outside reality of the novel. Coral with her wine-glass, in the priest's last dream, is meant to tell us that he is saved. Greene has a weakness for dreams. The wink would have been enough.

The Power and the Glory illustrates the maxim that 'one can't hand in a resignation to God', in its priest, unworthy by human standards, who persists in his duty without expecting a reward; and in its Mexico, absurdly attempting to resign. *Brighton Rock* shows in Pinkie that the devil accepts no resignations. *The Heart*

of the Matter (1948) is the story of a loyal servant of God who
resigns, without any thought of the devil, with what he considers
the best intentions. Whether the resignation is accepted remains
unclear. It has vexed readers because it is powerful but worrying
on this point. Evelyn Waugh's review for *The Tablet* observed
that 'the reader is haunted by the question Is Scobie damned?
One does not really worry very much whether Becky Sharp or
Fagin is damned. It is the central question of "The Heart of the
Matter".'[75] An atheist might say that the novel shows how
absurd the question is; but an atheist susceptible to fiction
would worry because a good novel creates its own laws and
Scobie has a soul to be lost or won. A serious objection, brought
by Ian Gregor against *The End of the Affair* and equally
applicable to its predecessor, is that we ought to know, because
a novelist is omniscient in his own book:[76] Greene surrenders his
decision to God but Scobie's soul is subject only to the novel's
laws; the last judgement on him should be there. Novels ought
not to raise a central question and leave it unanswered.

We worry because Scobie is likeable. According to Greene's
Introduction he was meant to be a portrait of a man corrupted
by pity. He notes that he 'touched on' the theme in his
'entertainment', *The Ministry of Fear* (1943), and he quotes from
there: 'Pity is cruel. Pity destroys. Love isn't safe when
pity's prowling round' (4.1.3). Scobie's pity, he comments,
arises from a 'monstrous pride'.[77] Since the absence of pity can
express the same thing, 'pity' means 'false pity', of the kind of
which Fowler, the narrator of *The Quiet American*, accuses
himself: his is a selfish pity by which he protects himself from
the pain of others (2.1.4). Greene complains that readers 'ex-
onerated' Scobie: 'Scobie was [to them] 'a good man who
was hunted to his doom by the harshness of his wife'.[78] The
Scobie of the novel is 'Scobie the Just', a man who tries to be a
just rather than a good man. His wife and his confessor, at the
end, judge him to have loved God but nobody else. He cannot
bear the sufferings of others in just the way explained by
Fowler, but unlike Fowler he is too stupid to see it. The earlier
novels warn us to mistrust a Greene character who believes in
human justice. Scobie's selfish pity and stupidity are apparent
and the pity commented on throughout the story but, even so,
Greene allows us to take his side.

Scobie is a police officer in British colonial West Africa. In a key scene, he visits a hospital and is asked by Mrs Bowles, the missionary in charge, to read to a convalescent small boy from *A Bishop Among the Bantus*, an improving book unlikely to entertain. The boy, who is hoping for a pirate story, does not understand the title. A sensible man in Scobie's position would say that the book was rather dull but he would tell a pirate story instead. Scobie improvises a tale of pirates called Bantus pursued by Arthur Bishop.

> Can it be, Arthur Bishop wondered, that I am about to meet the object of my quest, Blackbeard, the leader of the Bantus himself, or his blood-thirsty lieutenant . . . Batty Davis, so called because of his insane rages when he would send a whole ship's crew to the plank? (2.1.1.4)

Integrity makes him devious: he stays as close to his promise to read this book as his pity for the disappointed child he imagines will allow. The missionary is to read tomorrow. The fact that the boy, who enjoys today's reading, will look forward to the next episode, and that his relations with Mrs Bowles, who disapproves of fiction, will be at least strained, does not occur to Scobie. This is the best of the relatively few comic scenes in the novel, but the comedy does not bring out Scobie's folly; rather, he plays the comedy at Mrs Bowles's expense. Only one sentence hints at the small disaster he has prepared. He says, 'Of course it may sound a bit different when she reads it'. The rest of the scene makes him a sympathetic, avuncular figure, harassed by Mrs Bowles.

The novel harasses Scobie from the beginning, and the well contrived plot hounds him to a tragic breakdown. His wife Louise is pitiless in tormenting him; unable to see how she enjoys it, he blames himself. Their relations are a fine study in the strength of her weakness and the weakness in the strength with which he puts up with her. He has been passed over for Commissioner and she nags him to find the money for her to take a holiday in South Africa; how he does it is 'man's business', she says. Also good is Scobie's relationship with Yusuf the Syrian trader from whom he borrows the money. Yusuf is unctuous in admiration for Scobie's integrity ('A Daniel has come to the Colonial Police') and in yearning for friendship; he exploits his advantage until he controls his 'friend', but Greene hints at a trace of respect far back in

Yusuf's commercial soul. A young widow from a torpedoed ship overhears his story of the Bantus and, his wife away, they become friends; to protect her from a cad called Bagster he becomes her lover, in dutiful adultery. His wife's return makes his situation impossible. Yusuf has a letter Scobie has written to Helen and threatens to use it. His wife requires him to take communion; unable to make a good confession because he pities Helen, he 'insults' God by taking communion without having confessed, and drifts from mortal sin into what his normal state of mind would call heretical nonsense. He kills himself pitying God, and accepting damnation for the sake of his wife and mistress. Circumstances and the people about him are so ruthless that we sympathise when we should be watching the menace to love in his tragic flaw.

To pity God is, surely, for a Catholic, 'monstrous pride' and it ought to make Scobie ridiculous. His attitude, in the last stages praying 'O God, I offer up my damnation to you. Take it. Use it for them' (3.1.2.2), ought to be more obviously absurd; and by now we should be accustomed to finding him ridiculous. Instead we may well decide either that the climate of the Coast has unhinged his mind, or that there is a mad saintliness in his suicide, an ultimate appeal to God. Greene seems to relish the erosion of Scobie's integrity. 'You are too good to live', says Wilson the young secret-service man, a rather needless character, who spies on him. Indeed he is perhaps a better man when reduced to half-collusion in Yusuf's murder of his faithful servant Ali, than when he was Scobie the Just. The novel's epigraph is from Péguy:

Le Pécheur est au coeur même de chrétienté ... Nul n'est aussi compétent que le pêcheur en matière de chrétienté. Nul, si ce n'est le saint.

'Only, perhaps, the saint is as "competent" in Christianity as the sinner, who is at the very heart of the matter.' This paradoxical thought proved very dangerous in the Middle Ages wherever it led to the idea that a good Christian ought to sin. Since Scobie becomes more successful when in mortal sin, appointed Commissioner after all, that idea was not presumably in Greene's mind. But he is always attracted by paradox, by the nearness of opposites and the giddy line between sinner and saint. Péguy deliberately risked damnation in the cause of the damned.

The end of *The Heart of the Matter* leaves us unsure what to think, except that it is a fine novel hunting its hero remorselessly to destruction, full of fine portrayals of unpleasant people and creating a poetry of the humid, shabby West African setting where Greene had spent the last years of the war. It differs from *Brighton Rock* and *The Power and the Glory* in its relative humourlessness. When one amusing moment comes, Greene uncharacteristically explains it away. Yusuf talks about trust: '"One must always have boys one trusts. You must know more about them than they do about you." That apparently was his conception of trust' (3.1.4.1). The last reflection perhaps shows that Scobie is humourless, and strangely unaccustomed still to Syrian traders; but there is no need for it. Scobie is almost untouched by the dark comedy which helps to place the humourless Pinkie and gives life and resilience to the whisky-priest. He might have been tragi-comic, ridiculous in pride and pity, touching in his doom, grieving for God as he sent himself to hell. Much closer to our sympathy than such a character could be, Scobie is merely an appalling figure, worrying and unsatisfying in the end.[79]

Greene says that he considered withholding *The End of the Affair* (1951) from publication, but accepted a friend's advice to 'publish the bad as well as the good'.[80] The central question is less clear than in earlier novels and can be stated in a number of ways, of which the most reliable is 'the impossibility of disbelieving in God'. Bendrix, the novelist-narrator of this earliest of Greene's first-person novels, has been an atheist and now hates, resents and fears God because his former mistress, Sarah, has kept a vow she made to end the affair, when Bendrix appeared to be fatally injured. Since the vow she has gradually fallen in love with God with a passion which leads her to sainthood, confirmed by miracles after she dies.

Perhaps this book should have been a religious meditation rather than a novel. It is difficult to relate the characters' ideas to what happens, or to their relationships with one another; a reader may well decide that Greene was unsure of them. He may have thought some confusion justified by the tides of human and divine loves and hatreds which he meant to flow

through Bendrix's story and Sarah's diary (which forms Book
Three). At its best moments *The End of the Affair* glimpses
Greene's God, hungry for human love but as mysterious in his
choice as a human lover, and more demanding. First Bendrix
hates Helen's devotion to God; then he comes to hate God.
Sometimes one suspects that the author is expressing through
his character a fear of his own.

> If I ever loved like that, it would be the end of everything.
> Loving you I had no appetite for food, I felt no lust for any
> other woman, but loving him there'd be no pleasure in
> anything at all with him away. I'd even lose my work, I'd cease
> to be Bendrix. Sarah, I'm afraid. (5.7)

Such phrases as 'with him away', which normally refer to
human loves, give an intimacy to thoughts of God – far removed
from his adjectival and melodramatic appearance at the end of
Brighton Rock – which gives an irreligious reader insight into the
sensibility of a believer. This is, none the less, more than any of
the other novels, a work of primary interest to Catholics; and
they will agree with Greene that the miracles ought to have
been more tactfully managed. There is a danger, here, of
readers laughing at the author. Whether they are amused by
the private investigator of seedy adulteries, Mr Parkis, who
'educates' his twelve-year-old son in his trade, while the boy
imagines that his father is a Sexton Blake, is a matter of taste.
Some may be estranged from the grotesque parts of the novel in
which Parkis and his boy investigate Sarah; others may think
that the joke wears very thin. Something seems to have failed in
Greene's sense of humour here. That may help to explain the
awkward handling of the novel's miracles, and a general absence
of the creative energy of the best of the earlier books.

4

Discovering Comedy

Discussing *A Burnt-Out Case*, Greene says of his critics, 'they were too concerned with faith or no faith to notice that in the course of the blackest book I have written I had discovered Comedy'.[81] The central characteristic of his early work, the ambiguous nature of the absurd, of jokes which cannot quite amuse and mishaps which almost can, develops in the four major post-war novels, *The Quiet American* (1956), *A Burnt-Out Case* (1960), *The Comedians* (1966) and *The Honorary Consul* (1973) and becomes more complex. The quiet American, Pyle, is what Scobie or Bendrix might have been, a comic character who is frightening because he is unaware of what makes him comic, and because the trouble he causes blackens his humour, stressing that comedy depends on one's point of view. Monstrously funny, humourless characters appear, again causing catastrophes, in *A Burnt-Out Case*. These are comic creations of the same species as Anthony Powell's Widmerpool in *A Dance to the Music of Time*; *A Burnt-Out Case* introduces, by implication, the idea, fundamental in Powell and pervasive in British fiction, that a sense of humour is an essential feature of a sane mind. *The Comedians* is a very funny novel in which characters who have little or no sense of humour are treated sympathetically and from the point of view of a cynically amused narrator, obsessed with the ambiguous nature of comedy. Greene has complained about critics who use 'Greeneland' as a label limiting the world of his novels to a strange, violent 'seedy region of the mind'. He has claimed the 'tragi-comic region of La Mancha', and in these novels he makes it too extensive for any label to limit.[82]

The dedication describes *The Quiet American* as 'a story and not a piece of history', and it is a kind of detective story. A

young American, Pyle, from the embassy but widely known to
be CIA, has been murdered in French Saigon one night in the
early 1950s, and the narrator, Thomas Fowler, is ordered to the
Sûreté, with his mistress the lovely young Phuong, to answer
questions. 'Not guilty', he tells the French police-chief Vigot,
but 'I told myself that it was true' raises a doubt (1.1). 'No one
but Pyle was responsible', he decides a moment later. The story
which follows is less Vigot's than Fowler's, which time-shifts in
the narrative allow the criminal inquiry to parallel; 'Not guilty'
becomes a larger issue than a policeman can manage. Fowler
reconstructs his relationship with Pyle, as a rival for Phuong
who left him for Pyle and now returns, as a kind of friend, and
as an opponent, in whose death he is implicated, in the struggle
for Vietnam. In the last words of the novel, Fowler admits
guilt, although the appeal is to God, not to human justice. As
in a detective story, everything looks different on second
reading. We see then how much Fowler conceals in the first
chapter, and how the full story gradually filters through his
narrative, which is both a confession and a case for the defence.

The novel includes reports on the French war in Vietnam
which are based on four visits Greene made to the country
between 1951 and 1955.[83] The episodes in which a sceptical
English newsman goes up-country for news are well integrated
in the novel.

> For a moment I didn't see what they had seen, but when I
> saw, my mind went back, I don't know why to the Chalet
> and the female impersonators and the young soldiers whistling
> and Pyle saying, 'This isn't a bit suitable.'
> The canal was full of bodies. (1.4.1)

Pyle's comment is one to remember. Fowler witnesses this
particular massacre outside Phat Diem, on patrol with a French
unit. Pyle arrives that night to announce that he is in love with
Phuong. Fowler's next sortie is to Tanyin, stronghold of the
Caodaists who practise a religion, based on Buddhism,
Christianity and Confucius, which the novel presents as
diverting nonsense: 'In the Caodaist faith all truths are reconciled
and truth is love.' Pyle has confidence in these 'friendly' people,
who are one of many embattled forces competing in the
countryside. Fowler warns him:

'The French don't trust them.'
Pyle said solemnly, 'A man becomes trustworthy when you trust him.' It sounded like a Caodaist maxim. (2.2)

It fails on this occasion; in consequence they have a narrow escape from the Vietminh, Pyle further vexing Fowler by saving his life. At Haiphong in a later scene, a French pilot takes Fowler on a vertical raid, vividly remembered from Greene's experience of such a flight, on a village in the north, and afterwards describes the waste of life, in the napalmed villages and in the French officer corps which takes very heavy losses in a cause it knows is lost. Back in Saigon, a spate of small bicycle-bomb attacks is followed by an explosion causing serious loss of life (the novel reverses the order of real events of 1951 and 1952); Fowler discovers that Pyle has supplied the arms to a terrorist group with a view to forming an American 'third force'.

The character whom Greene involves in the catastrophe of Vietnam is on first encounter a figure of light comedy, a naïve and sentimental lover. Pyle is socially inept: 'He had a way of staring hard at a girl as though he hadn't seen one before and then blushing' (1.3.1). When he dances with Phuong he holds her 'so far away that you expected him at any moment to sever contact' (1.3.2). Although a Harvard man, he is not bright. When the tedious Miss Hei, ambitious for a good husband for her younger sister, 'the most beautiful girl in Saigon', talks flatly and at length about Phuong's conventional virtues, Fowler laughs; Pyle looks shocked, 'and suddenly it occurred to me that he was genuinely interested in what she had to say' (1.3.2). That tone of ironic amusement, increasingly touched by pained annoyance that Pyle should take himself seriously, marks Fowler's account of how he lost Phuong to so unprepossessing a suitor.

Pyle is insensitive to nuance in speech, and tone-deaf to British English. He catches something of Fowler's cynicism but none of his irony. At the end of this first evening with Fowler and Phuong, when shocked by the transvestite dancers, he says 'Fowler, let's go. We've had enough haven't we? This isn't a bit suitable for *her*?' He cannot hear how the stress, his first encroachment on his host's relationship, will sound. Some people may be said to 'colonise' others. He means to colonise

Phuong and make a good, quiet American wife of her, but he also colonises Fowler. His 'haven't we?' is the first sign of it. When he announces that he is in love with Phuong, he says in apology that he 'wouldn't ever come between a man and his wife' – Fowler's English wife has refused him a divorce.

'I can call you Tom, can't I? I feel in a way that this has brought us together. Loving the same woman, I mean.'

Fowler makes no comment on that, except to prefer 'Thomas' and continue to say 'Pyle'.

But there was a quality of the implacable in Pyle. He had determined that I was behaving well and I had to behave well. He said, 'I know what you are suffering, Thomas.'
'I'm not suffering.'
'Oh yes, you are. I know what I'd suffer if I had to give up Phuong.' (1.4.2)

Here and throughout the novel he explains to his 'best friend' Tom that his only thought is Phuong's happiness. His egotism creates a 'straight', 'honourable' version of Fowler which suits him. He is sure that Tom must want what is best for Phuong, and although Tom will suffer, he can be sure of a friend's sympathy.

Pyle's implacability also appears when he is fighting for democracy. The traditional parallel between soldier and lover is frequently mentioned, and sometimes implied as when Fowler refers to a woman's 'field of battle' (3.2.2). Pyle's stupidity and wilful confidence, which Fowler calls 'innocence' and presents with a fine balance between amusement and exasperation when Pyle takes over Phuong, are strongly established in these 'love scenes'. They strengthen the case, when he starts to take over Saigon, that his enemies in the war are right to kill him. The Communist Mr Heng tells Fowler that 'we would talk to him' (4.2.1). It is obvious from Pyle's arguments over Phuong that talking to him is a waste of time. Invincible 'innocence' shows its sinister possibilities when Fowler and Pyle are trapped at night with two young Vietnamese in a watchtower in Viet-held territory. Pyle talks about his ideas, derived from an American writer called York Harding whose books he cherishes, for making

Asia safe for democracy. Fowler, who is on principle uncommitted, puts various objections which are in effect ignored. When the Viets approach the tower, Pyle turns from his benign abstractions about Asia to the practical problem of the two young Asians. '"And these?" Pyle asked, and he added with a shocking directness, "Shall I shoot them?" Perhaps he wanted to try the sten' (2.2.3).

Greene approves of implacability, in Catholic martyrs for example, and of commitment even in a dubious cause. The neutral Fowler's narrative has to allow for the attraction of youthful enthusiasm and strength of purpose in Pyle, while condemning 'innocence' – the inability to see the horror which should humble us. Dead soldiers signify only 'war'; when he sees the results of his bomb in Saigon, Pyle is shocked but still unable to apprehend. There is blood on his shoes, and he says he will have to clean them before he sees the Minister. 'I don't think he knew what he was saying', Fowler comments. He cannot persuade Pyle that the dying civilians are his responsibility.

> Indeed I had said too much already. He looked white and beaten and ready to faint, and I thought, 'What's the good? He'll always be an innocent, you can't blame the innocent, they are always guiltless. All you can do is control them, or eliminate them. Innocence is a kind of insanity. (3.2.2)

Where indifference is opposed to commitment, in the rivalry for Phuong, Fowler grudgingly concedes that his cynicism is inferior; but the novel highlights innocence, and the voice of experience, in these definite lines, obviously has the author's approval.

Henry James's Americans tend to be innocent and moral in contrast to experienced, cynical Europeans. But Greene's American has none of the strength of this Jamesian innocence. The fine Puritan traditions of James's New England have been replaced, in Greene's view, by a dubious academic world where Pyle has studied ' – well, one of those subjects Americans can take degrees in: perhaps public relations or theatrecraft, perhaps even Far Eastern studies' (1.1). The novel is hostile to American policy in Indo-China; Fowler dislikes everything American. Joe, the Economic Attaché and officially Pyle's boss, looks like 'a face on television' or 'the man who keeps his friends because he uses the right deodorants' (1.3.1). Like Pyle, Joe pays no attention to remarks he does not like. His thoughts are mechanically conventional and Fowler baffles him. None of these characters – from the country of Lincoln and Mark Twain – can understand irony or appreciate any but the simplest tones of voice. Pyle is 'quiet' because the others shout and brawl in public places. The noisiest, a journalist called Granger, replies to Fowler's abuse, at the end of the book. But Fowler is allowed to shape aphorisms – 'as ill-designed as the Statue of Liberty and as meaningless'. Granger is not – 'I don't like Limies. . . . You all talk like poufs. You're so damned superior. You think you know everything' (4.2.4). Fowler, who quotes Baudelaire and understands Pascal, knows far more than any of the Americans, even about sex (2.2.3). The novel makes no hint that Fowler is unfair, except, perhaps, when he draws attention to the 'associations' of Pyle's name. On the contrary, rather than introduce English types of innocence or smugness, Greene supplies worldly, cultured Frenchmen, and beautifully civilised Vietnamese.

It may be that the portrait of Pyle and the case against American policy are weakened by the bias of this satire. But it is among the liveliest attacks on the speech and manners of Americans in modern literature. In the scene where Granger and Fowler talk (4.2.4), they reach a rough sense of human fellowship, caused by Granger's distress over his child's polio, and they seem to belong to cultures which are quite alien but allied. Granger loathes Limies but would rather talk to one now than to 'those Frogs', because at least Limies speak 'a kind of English'. The bond of a common language, whatever the cultural differences, and the solace it offers in an emergency, are well observed here, which strengthens the point that, like Pyle, Fowler has failed to recognise in Granger 'the mess of life'.

The author's Catholicism is muted in this novel, but it remains distinct, and non-Catholic readers may feel as strong a bias against them as before. The most attractive character is the policeman Vigot – unless Phuong, lovely and obedient as she tends Fowler's pipes of opium, can be called a character. Vigot has no innocent faith in human justice, but his passion for finding the truth is an artist's. He wins always at *Quatre Cent*

Vingt-et-un, the French bar-game for which he has invented a sexual argot, exclaiming '*Sans vaseline*' when the dice fall (4.2.1). His 'miserable smile', toughness, intelligence and liking for risks including 'the risk of God' – from his favourite author Pascal – all recommend him to those who know a good man in Greene; like almost all the approved characters in the novels, Vigot drinks *au sérieux*, proposing *vermouth cassis* when even Fowler thinks it too early. At almost every point the opposite of Pyle, he is, of course, a Catholic.

Catholicism is mentioned every few pages. When Fowler explains his dislike of the idea of confession to a priest at Phat Diem, the answer is 'I don't suppose you've ever had much to regret' (1.4.1). Although supposedly indifferent, Fowler broods about religion, noticing points, sometimes with approval. Seeing a dead child with a holy medal, he tells himself 'the juju doesn't work' (1.4.1). Later he reflects that 'no human being will ever understand another' and thinks that is the reason 'why men have invented God – a being capable of understanding' (1.4.2). At the end of the story he has something to regret. Mr Heng has asked Fowler to invite Pyle to dinner at the Vieux Moulin, where men can conveniently 'talk to him', and dump the corpse discreetly in the canal. Undecided when talking to Pyle that evening, he leaves the invitation open. 'I handed back the decision to that Somebody in whom I didn't believe: You can intervene if You want to: a telegraph on his desk: a message from the Minister' (4.2.3). Like 'the juju doesn't work' this looks planted by the author, Fowler is deliberately more naïve than we should expect about the nature of the Somebody he calls to mind. Later in the evening and sure that Pyle has been killed, he feels that by co-operating with Heng he has lost his neutrality: 'I had become as engagé as Pyle, and it seemed to me that no decision would ever be simple again'; when Granger looks aggressive he wouldn't mind being 'beaten unconscious' because 'we have so few ways in which to assuage the sense of guilt' (4.2.4). At the end, all is well; his wife has promised a divorce and he is to marry Phuong. But 'how I wished there existed someone to whom I could say I was sorry'. The words of the priest at Phat Diem are more noticeable on a second reading of the novel, which is, not quite unobtrusively, written from a Catholic point of view, and told by a narrator who seems less safe from Greene's Somebody than he admits.

The book's best achievement is not Fowler's self-portrait, or thoughts on God, or war-reporting – though this is of the highest quality – but the comic figure of Pyle seen in relation to the rest, and especially to the horrors of war. If he is simplified into farce, so are the events in Vietnam. Fowler's reporting looks at appearances – bodies in the canal – for he is, he says, a reporter not a leader writer. He remembers Pyle without attempting depth-psychology, although he concedes that the young man's sorrow in the House of the Five Hundred Girls – 'They were so pretty' – is a true regret for corruption, which hints at something beyond the superficial absurdity. Whatever that might be, it is less worth attention than Pyle the buffoon, beautifully brought to life in the scene where he calls to propose to Phuong. The novel's structure, which tells us at the start that he has died a victim of his innocence, gives a pattern to his clowning.

Fowler is the ideal Pyle-watcher: 'I noticed that his crew-cut had recently been trimmed' (2.1). His 'Thomas' is a declaration, Fowler decides, that he is 'here to get Phuong', catching just the way Pyle uses sincerity as a weapon. Phuong's English is limited, like Pyle's French. Fowler interprets, 'with meticulous care – it sounded worse that way'.

> 'Has she understood that?' he asked.
> 'As far as I can tell. You don't want me to add a little fire to it do you?'
> 'Oh no', he said, 'just translate. I don't want to sway her emotionally.'

After a while it occurs to him that this is an odd situation. 'Me asking you to translate.' When Fowler expresses surprise at the medical information submitted in the proposal, including blood-group, Pyle senses the surface of a mockery he cannot begin to fathom: 'Don't laugh at me, Thomas. I expect I'm old fashioned.' Fowler suggests that it would be simpler to 'dice for her'. 'Now you are pretending to be tough, Thomas.' The idea of someone 'too innocent to live' returns, on reading this scene, if we recall Pyle briefing Congressmen, or the dead bodies in the canal. Impervious to irony, unconscious of a culture other than his own, whether Phuong's or that which values novels (as he, Fowler notes, does not), determined to have her and her country for their own good, Pyle is a hero of our time. Against a tragic background more apt than Greene knew in 1956, he is seen in the right perspectives.

The dangers of 'innocence' are not forgotten in *A Burnt-Out Case* (1959), but its main theme is the evil of worldly success. At the leper colony in the Upper (Belgian) Congo where the famous Catholic architect Querry seeks asylum from the world, a burnt-out case is a leper whose disease has left him mutilated but cured. Querry and the doctor, Colin, discuss parallels between such a position and his ennui. Colin is an atheist, Querry a Catholic who no longer believes; perhaps religion is a disease; Querry sometimes thinks that all involvement in life is 'contagious', and that he is no longer a danger. But such ennui is another type of illness. At the end, Colin pronounces a post-mortem.

> He had been cured of all but his success; but you can't cure success, any more than I can give my *mutilés* back their fingers and toes. . . . Success is like that too – a mutilation of the natural man. (6.3.6)

'Success' in this sense is not achievement. Dr Colin works hard to cure lepers. The journalist Parkinson, who 'discovers' the new Schweitzer-like Querry, can bestow or withhold leprous success through the millions of readers of his syndicated articles. 'Fame' is not quite a synonym, for Querry's is based on solid achievements, but he has little respect for public or expert opinion about his art. The novel is developed from ideas which are commonplace among world-famous people today; the public hero, like the leper a victim of misfortune, may easily become an outcast too. Greene's gloom on this theme is worked into a dark comedy which is best in its studies of those unhappy enough to envy success and enjoy it vicariously where they can. They are, in the novel's leading metaphor, the leprophils.

The plot is a series of ironies. Querry's flight into obscurity makes him more famous than ever before, in the world which reads Parkinson, and more keenly tormented by admirers. He settles among the lepers because he is tired of humanity, yet soon wins a reputation as a great humanitarian – increased when he goes into the bush one night, too indifferent for fear,

to rescue his leper-servant, a burnt-out *mutilé* (who happens to
be called Deo Gratias). The intellectual Catholic layman
Rycker, a businessman down river, and Father Thomas, the
keenest theologian in the religious community which runs the
colony, to both of whom Querry explains his complete
indifference to God and man, spread his reputation as a saint.
Querry has also been famous as a womaniser, though lust has
now died with all other desires (except for whisky, of which he
has brought an apparently inexhaustible supply, and cigarettes).
Innocently, Rycker sends his very young and unloving wife to
lure the great man into visiting. Rycker gives Parkinson a
splash-story about Querry's saintly expiation of a sinful lifetime.
Later Querry spends a blameless night in the town of Luc with
Madame Rycker. She learns there that she is pregnant, and
seeing no other way to escape from her unhappy marriage, tells
her husband, now suspicious of Querry, that he seduced her
months ago. For the first time in all his dealings with women,
he is blameless – except for having made the basic mistake of
pitying an innocent. The 'good Catholic' Rycker, knowing that
no Belgian jury will convict after such a *crime passionnel*, shoots
and kills him. Parkinson's next story is 'The Saint who Failed'.

Greene had written for the theatre during the 1950s. As in a
well made stage-play, the characters unwittingly prepare for
ironies to come. When the Superior tells Querry that Madame
Rycker has been 'sent' by her husband he asks, 'Is that the
custom here? Tell him I'm not interested' (3.2). Protesting to
Parkinson about Rycker's obsession with his saintliness, Querry
says 'My God, I'm almost tempted to seduce his wife. That at
least might change his tune' (4.3.2). Even the Fathers notice
that the final events resemble 'one of those Palais Royal farces
that one has read . . . the injured husband pops in and out'
(6.3.4). The comic aspect of his predicament occurs to Querry
when Rycker is brandishing his gun; and Rycker shoots him
because he laughs.

Greene's fiction may be said to have discovered laughter in *A
Burnt-Out Case*. In the earlier novels laughter is usually cruel
and primitive, the children mocking Padre José, American
reporters guffawing in restaurants. That loud, open laughter is
at the expense of others. A pained smile is preferable. The
whisky-priest quietly giggles at himself, and Fowler smiles to
himself. But Querry revives from the lifeless condition in which

he arrives at the *léproserie* by learning to laugh. In this novel, a smile can be sinister, a sign of all that is wrong with the smiler: 'Father Thomas . . . fetching up a smile like a liquorice-stick, dark and sweet and prehensile' (4.1.3).

At his most burnt-out, in the first chapter, Querry shrinks from laughter. The bishop's boat which brings him up to the *léproserie* (and goes no further), stops at a seminary where the priests laugh among themselves. He finds this irritating 'like a noisy child or a disc of jazz' (1.1.2). 'The passenger wondered when it was that he had first begun to detest laughter like a bad smell.' Hearing Africans laughing, he feels 'taunted', as though by 'the unknown syllables of an enemy tongue'. Unsure of his welcome, at the *léproserie* Querry says that he might go into the bush on foot; Dr Colin looks in vain for a smile (2.1.1). Dr Colin comes to recognise 'a twitch of the mouth' (4.1.1) as Querry's equivalent to a smile (a broad smile, 'like an advertisement', is usually a bad sign in all the novels). Later, Querry finds Marie Rycker as easy to amuse as a child – she giggles – and although her innocence looks suspect, he is now at ease with jokes. At the 'feast' which celebrates the hospital's completion, he remembers the seminary of the first chapter and wonders at himself, relaxed among the laughing Fathers. Rejection of laughter is a bad sign. 'How dare he laugh at me?' Rycker demands when he has fired his gun, and Querry says 'laughing at myself' (6.3.6). Querry's last words, 'This is absurd . . . or else', are accompanied by 'a distorted laugh'. Distorted, effortful laughter appears an achievement to respect in contrast to the absence of comic sense in Rycker and Father Thomas.

'Querry' combines 'quest' and 'quarry'. Querry's quest is how to be human again, far away from success which reduced him to a bored, indifferent state in which he does not care what he does. Greene is interested by the idea that an absolutely selfish man might act selflessly. A simpler Catholic novel would have used the situation to show Providence leading Querry to the cure of his soul, advancing him by stages – friendship with Deo Gratias and Colin, hard work, community, daily sight of suffering – to the revival of a sound mind and a sure faith. Greene does not deny such a possibility. Colin tells Querry near the end of the novel, that he cannot claim to be an atheist because he is still troubled by the loss of his faith; at the end the Superior quotes Pascal: to look for God is to have found him.

But while Querry shows faint signs of a faith not quite extinct, Rycker and Thomas drive him further away from sympathy with their religion. Unhappy Catholics, they are hungry for a saint and he is their quarry.

Rycker was rejected by the Jesuits after six years of training, he tells us, and Parkinson discovers why: 'he can't bear not being important' (6.3.4). He speaks of his love of God in tones which imply a special relationship. God is 'He' in Rycker's speech because he pronounces the capital. He enlists God's authority to urge his reluctant young wife to her 'marital duties', and teaches her to love God to give himself 'some security'. Speaking of '*The* Querry', pronouncing the italics, and boasting of their spiritual friendship, gives him status, and he will not hear any denial from the man himself. Being a saint, he explains, means that 'you don't belong to yourself any more' (6.1.1). He is a caricature of the talk of unintelligent intellectual laymen whom religion has slightly crazed. The satire is often very funny:

'To tell you the truth', Rycker said, 'I find those fathers at the *léproserie* an unsatisfactory lot. They are more interested in electricity and building than in questions of faith.' (2.2)

At other times he is pathetic, running after the scowling Querry, or praising him eagerly to the bishop.

'– you must admit, Monseigneur, that self-sacrifices like that are rare. What do you think?'
    'I am wondering, does he play bridge?' (3.1.1)

He is pathetic because he cannot smile at that reply, or guess how funny he is; 'how dare he laugh at me?' are the perfect words for his tilt into mania.

In Rycker, religious complacency is a kind of madness. Father Thomas (aptly named) is a priest with doubts. When Querry declares his unbelief, Thomas feels uplifting solidarity with the distinguished Catholic. He and Rycker avoid the awkward point that their saint is a disbeliever by referring to the 'dark night of the soul' experienced by St John of the Cross, the final testing of a saint through 'aridity'.[84] In Thomas's best scene, where his smile is like liquorice, he complains of

sleeplessness, reinterprets all Querry says, and concludes with
thanks. Then, like Rycker, he claims Querry. '"I shall sleep
tonight", Father Thomas said, threateningly.' The threat is
that of a parasite who invents a relationship to boost self-
importance. Left in charge while the Superior is away, Thomas
thrives on authority, and this pleasure in success is marked by
lack of humour: 'he crumbled his bread with the closed face of
importance'. Greene has many ways to mock him. The scene in
which he shows Querry Parkinson's piece about the new
Schweitzer (5.2) contrasts with his immediate disillusion when
Marie Rycker makes her accusation. He is also placed by the
images which contain the author's comment. '"Ha, ha." Father
Thomas caught the joke in mid-air and confiscated it like a
schoolboy's ball under his soutane' (4.1.3). This comments on
Thomas and on schoolmasterliness.

Descriptive writing is much better in *A Burnt-Out Case* than in
the last two novels with foreign settings. *The Heart of the Matter*
labels Africa with faint adjectives, often in pairs: it is a 'strange
continent' (1.1.6); its roads are 'ugly and clay-heavy', its
harbour has 'black slow water' (1.1.6); a girl has 'a young black
African face' and 'a bright cotton frock' (1.1.2); early morning
brings 'flat cold light' (2.1.1.2) – later the light is 'gentle and
clear and fresh'; in one section, a priest lives in a 'dismal little'
house, close to 'decayed wooden settlers' huts'; Scobie dreams
of 'a wide cool meadow' in which there is a 'small green snake'.
A writer never out of England might have kept description as
vague as this. 'They moved down the red laterite slope on to
the raft, and then edged foot by foot across the dark styx-like
stream' (3.1.1.). Describing Phat Diem, Fowler mentions a
'long narrow street' which is 'packed and noisy'; it is a 'living'
town 'in its strange medieval way' (*QA* 1.4.2); in an aeroplane
he admires 'the huge majestic scenery' and the field of 'green
and grey' (3.1.4). *A Burnt-Out Case* observes more precisely,
from the start: the sudden brilliances of Africa appear in the
stream of butterflies 'tacking' into the boat, in the first chapter,
and the white nenuphars across the river look like 'a regiment
of swans'. Greene notices the shabby aspect of the grandest
tropical trees, 'brown at the top like stale cauliflowers' (2.1.1),
and how jungle greens are reflected in the river below the
'pewter' hue of the water. The smells of bush and swamp come
to Querry like 'a dentist's mask' (2.4.1).

Where the earlier novels are inclined to fuss about 'awful', 'hideous', 'dreadful' aspects of their worlds, this book is clinical about its lepers' deformities. It is good in stressing their normality. Dr Colin examines a child: 'his father accompanied him, and his fingerless fist rested on the boy's shoulder to give him comfort' (2.3.1). The presentation of the priests is equally vivid. They appeal to Greene because they are so unsuburban: they ask no questions; they are no more curious than the Foreign Legion would be about why Querry has fled.[85] They are more versatile than *légionnaires*, able to captain the bishop's boat or lecture on Greek. Sharp observation conveys the austerity of their life. The Superior, summoned by the bishop, packs his belongings into a knapsack and is ready to leave, perhaps for ever. He contemplates 'the bleak refectory in which he had spent his best years':

The buildings, wherever he went, would always be much the same. . . . There would always be the same coloured reproduction of the Pope's portrait, but this one had a stain in the corner where the leper who made the frame had spilt the walnut colouring. (5.1.2)

Greene had seen the bare uniformity of Congo *léproseries*. He sees here that for a mission-Father such minutiae as this stain are the signs of home.

A measured comedy is often present in the prose. In the opening paragraphs Querry comes up-river in the bishop's boat.

The passenger would be woken at four in the morning by the tinkling sound of the sanctus bell in the saloon, and presently from the window of the Bishop's cabin, which he shared with a crucifix, a chair, a table, a cupboard where cockroaches lurked, and one picture – the nostalgic photograph of some church in Europe covered in a soutane of heavy snow, he would see the congregation going home across the gang-plank. He would watch them as they climbed the steep bank and disappeared into the bush, swinging lanterns like the carol singers he had once seen during his stay in a New England village. By five the boat was on the move again, and at six as the sun rose he would eat his breakfast with the captain. The next three hours, before the great heat had begun, were for both men the best of the day, and the passenger found that he could watch, with a kind of inert content, the thick rapid, khaki-coloured stream against which the small boat fought its way at about three knots, the engine, somewhere below the altar and the Holy Family, groaning like an exhausted animal and the big wheel churning away at the stern.

The last sentence contrasts the boat's efforts with the passenger's inertia, and the boat's mechanical functions, which the metaphor makes animal, with its ecclesiastical role. Its quizzicality has been prepared for, by the mention of the altar and Holy Family as plain facts about the boat, convenient for locating the engine, as it might have been 'somewhere below the quarter-deck', so that the words take the place of nautical terms. 'The sanctus bell in the saloon', which sounds like a special ship's bell, is 'Greenean', in the way that a phrase may be quintessentially Dickensian; its combination of sacred and convivial associations is part of the subdued humour of the passage. Religious vocabulary in this sentence leads to the 'congregation' of African villagers going home from early mass, and then to the oddness of 'gang-plank'. The incongruity of the last term is more entertaining because of the matter-of-fact details which the complex sentence carefully gathers. 'Soutane of heavy snow' recalls the opening lines where 'the captain in a white soutane' begins the amused substitution of 'captain' for 'Father' or 'priest'.

The concentration of Greene's best writing appears in many ways. The comedy of colonial life is captured in one word, in the scene of the governor's party when the host is absent because 'he's gone to unlock some more whisky' (3.1.1). A deep distrust of Africans ('Never let your "boys" get at the whisky – they will steal it, drink it, revert to savagery') lurks in 'unlock'. It appears too in the images. Those already quoted with reference to Father Thomas discredit him in very small space. They work in both directions: a stick of liquorice and the schoolmaster's act of confiscation have never seemed so unpleasant as when Thomas 'fetches up' a smile or confiscates a joke. Querry prefers Parkinson to Rycker as a tormentor because the journalist has 'interstices in that cracked character where the truth might occasionally seed', whereas Rycker is 'like a wall so plastered over with church announcements that you couldn't even see the brickwork' (6.1.1). Church announcements seem discredited by that association. A 'cracked' character leads to the metaphor of brickwork appropriate to Rycker's dense impassivity.

Greene achieves the concentration of poetry, often finding sensory expression for abstract qualities or states of mind, or abstract likenesses for physical things. This has always been a feature of his writing: the whisky-priest drinks his brandy down 'like damnation'; Vigot's police station smells of 'urine and injustice' (*QA* 1.2.1). In this novel, where disorders of the body resemble those of the man within, such effects are common: 'the pouches under his eyes were like purses that contained the smuggled memories of a disappointing life' (2.1.3). 'Smuggled' is apt because the man is a customs officer; it makes the memories furtive – ashamed and imperfectly concealed. Marie Rycker remembers how her husband turned away from her, on their marriage night, once he was satisfied: 'the holy medal that he always wore had got twisted by their embrace and now lay in the small of his back, facing her like a reproach' (3.1.2). Exactly the right word for the purpose looks inevitable in such well-crafted writing: 'twisted' is literal and metaphorical, the medal like the man serving an unchristian Catholicism.

The novel contains another form of commentary in its aphorisms. Its first sentence adapts Descartes: 'I feel discomfort, therefore I am alive' is all that remains unburnt-out in Querry at the start. Thought soon revives, however. Some reflections are orthodox. 'Suffering is something which will always be provided when required', the Superior tells Querry (1.1.2). Dr Colin is given to tart epigrams. When the Superior regrets people's false fears about leprosy, he says, 'They learn it from the Bible, like sex' (1.2.2). Some comments are familiar from earlier Greene. 'God preserve us from all innocence', Querry exclaims, apropos Marie Rycker: 'at least the guilty know what they are about' (6.3.4). Most such remarks, however, are tentative judgements on the action. Thomas apart, the Fathers are too busy tending their lepers and running their church, to explain things. The Superior says that 'superficial' judgements are safer because they can be 'shrugged off' when they fail (1.2.2): he seems to combine Fowler's belief that nobody can really understand anyone else with the priestly thought (expressed by Father Rank at the end of *The Heart of the Matter*) that nobody knows just how God judges. Wisdom in this novel, and in those which followed, includes a measure of scepticism about the value of reason and its connection with faith. Father Jean, we are told, used to be 'a brilliant moral theologian' but now poses as a film-fan, 'as though it would help him to wipe out an ugly past' (4.1.2). Jean introduces the idea that comedy provides a clue to God's nature. Comparing Rycker, at the end, to the injured husband in a farce, he suggests that 'God was not entirely serious when he gave man the sexual instinct', and refers to St Thomas Aquinas who said that God 'made the world in play' (6.3.4).

Such interesting and to a strict Catholic (Evelyn Waugh, for example, whom the novel angered) dangerous ideas abound in Greene's work, increasingly heretical in characters in the later books. His gift is for neat, memorable formulations rather than original ideas or sustained thought. Had the priesthood claimed him after his conversion, he might have become an amusing, stimulating lecturer in theology, likely to be in trouble with his superiors. Although the author's religious orthodoxy is irrelevant to literary assessment, it is a tribute to the peculiar power of Greene's fiction that such improper interest is hard to exclude. There is no question about the novel's spirit of religious enquiry. Querry's death is the end of his story for Dr Colin, talking to the Superior:

'You can hardly say it was a happy ending for Querry.'
'Wasn't it? Surely he always wanted to go a bit farther.'
(6.3.6)

Querry constantly worries about his lost faith and so does the novel. The fairy-story he tells Marie when they pass the night together discredits 'the King' who stands for God, but afterwards he tells himself 'The King is dead, long live the King' (6.1.2). He is buried in the cemetery's atheists' corner; Deo Gratias lays a pagan offering there. But how wrong Catholics can be is one of the major themes. Deo Gratias, seeker of the happy place Pendele, knows before Querry is killed that he is to 'leave' and wants to go with him. Colin is given the last words which imply belief in commitment for its own sake, but the Superior has argued in his sermon (4.1.1) that if God exists, every life is for or against him. The Superior and Father John are closest to the outlook of the novel, which would vex a Thomas or a Rycker, but seem pointless to a Dr Colin.

W. B. Yeats distinguished between rhetoric which argues with others and poetry which argues with itself. Greene's earlier novels are rhetorical, in this sense; they are attacks upon complacency, indifference, innocence, written with indignation and saved at times from something like fanaticism by their sense of humour. *A Burnt-Out Case* explores its hero's 'indifference' in such a way that the term ceases to be a category which contains him as 'innocence' contains Pyle or 'complacency' Ida Arnold. *The Comedians* achieves poetry in its hesitation about the two innocents at the heart of the story; introduced as figures of fun, they grow into comic characters who, although ridiculous, are not undignified. There is an advance in Greene's kind of comedy here, although no relaxation of the tragic sense of life.

As fully as any earlier novel, *The Comedians* declines to look on the bright side of anything – its world is meant to dizzy and appal. Haiti in 1963 was suffering a reign of terror under 'Papa Doc' Duvalier which had, temporarily, driven out the British and American ambassadors and the Papal nuncio. Greene's first object was to urge that they should not return.[86] He began with the ploy used in *Stamboul Train*, showing frivolous foreigners against a reality of political evil. The non-Haitian characters are named as if in a comic anecdote: Brown, Jones and Smith. Brown owns a hotel which flourished in better times but is now empty; he hates Papa Doc for keeping the tourists away. Jones dreams of a 'good life' as future owner of a 'class' golf club. Mr and Mrs Smith have come from Wisconsin to establish a vegetarian centre. The Haitians suffer and resist Duvalier's tyranny. The hotel servant Joseph, who has been interrogated by the President's bogey-men, the 'Tontons Macoute', still limps. The poet Philipot, whose uncle has been driven to suicide, tries to form a guerrilla force. Dr Magiot, a Communist, cannot expect to live long. Westerners seem decadent and detached from the third world pitted against horrors. But the innocent Smiths, the indifferent Brown, and Jones in whom innocence and indifference mingle with fantasies, become involved in Haiti's tragedy and there are moments when they speak with an authority earned in the action. This counts more than the pronouncements of Dr Magiot which summarise Greene's principle of commitment. The novel is most effective when its 'comedians' begin, at least, to learn about 'tragedy' – where neutrality ends.

Brown, the narrator, is obsessed by thoughts of comedy and tragedy. As a boy at the Jesuit College of the Visitation, in Monte Carlo, his belief in God was 'a very serious affair': 'I saw Him incarnated in every tragedy.'

> Now that I approached the end of life it was only my sense of humour that enabled me sometimes to believe in Him. Life was a comedy, not the tragedy for which I had been prepared, and it seemed to me that we were all . . . driven by an authoritarian practical joker towards the extreme point of comedy. How often, in the crowd on Shaftesbury Avenue or Broadway, after the theatres closed, have I heard the phrase – I laughed till the tears came. (1.1.5)

The idea of an extreme point of comedy which brings tears is to be kept in mind, but Brown's story is more often one of comical events which turn macabre. Brown is like Querry, a lapsed Catholic who finds laughter difficult, but has a rueful sense of the absurd. Sarcasm helps him to live with conditions in Haiti. Wondering how the Secretary for Education hopes to fulfil his 'six-year plan to eliminate illiteracy in the north', he reminds himself that Hurricane Hazel in '54 had eliminated a great deal of illiteracy in the interior (1.4.2). The Tontons arrive to disrupt a funeral driving 'a big Cadillac dating from the days of American aid for the poor of Haiti' (1.5.1). He is inclined to tease the Smiths, pointing out that most Haitians are too poor to be carnivorous; but their sincerity shames him. Cynicism is cheap today, he tells himself – available at any Monoprix store 'built into all poor-quality goods' (1.1.3). He has not reached the 'laughter of despair' which he detects in the 'hilarity' of Petit Pierre, a journalist and Tonton informer, nor the 'courage and humour of the defeated' which he sees in the British chargé who carries dark glasses to mock the Tontons' use of them as uniform. Brown's humour is defensive and sour.

Most of the plot concerns Jones's attempt to pose as an arms dealer and defraud Papa Doc. He arrives with a letter of

introduction to someone in the army – a mistake since the
officers have taken refuge in foreign embassies. Brown and
Smith find him in a police cell, badly beaten-up but still
confident. When Brown sees him again he is in favour with the
Tonton captain, Concasseur. His scheme fails when Concasseur
goes to America to check on the arms, which do not exist.
Jones, who has hoped to buy his complicity, but badly mistimed
it, takes refuge with the South American ambassador whose
wife Martha is Brown's mistress. Brown becomes jealous and
exploits Jones's dubious boasting about his experience as a
major of commandos in the Far East during the war, persuading
him to lead Philipot's small ill-equipped band in the hills.
Although Jones has no experience of war, except as a civilian
entertaining troops, he agrees. The guerrillas kill Concasseur
but achieve little more. When Brown meets Philipot crossing
the border into the Dominican Republic (where he has already
taken refuge), he learns that Jones's flat feet have held him
back and that he has died covering his men's retreat. An
absurd figure has become a sort of hero by involvement, even if
almost by accident.

   Jones is a comedian in the French sense, of which Brown is
very conscious: an actor on life's stage, an adventurer, or 'tart'
in his own slang. He mingles the lies his fraud requires with
copious fantasies, so inexpertly – often contradicting himself –
that Brown is amused by the extent to which everyone else
believes him, though baffled by his power to make others laugh.
On the run from the Tontons, he appeals to Brown who takes
him to the *Medea*, the ominously-named Dutch ship which
brought them with the Smiths from America. Unable to remain
on board he dresses as a woman, in a costume from the purser's
theatre-box; Brown escorts him to Martha's embassy. Jones is
at his most attractive and amusing in these scenes, relishing his
latest role, making eyes at the Tonton who guards the gang-
plank, and entering diplomatic sanctuary on the ambassador's
arm. Watching him as he moves 'magnificently across the hall
like a Victorian matron', Martha laughs 'till her eyes filled
with tears' (3.1.1). His humour is unsophisticated. 'Major
Jones,' he insists. 'In the women's army of course.' Not exactly
brave, he makes rashness appealing by a childish zest and a
disregard for the hopelessness of his predicament. He is a
failure at almost everything – how much so appears in the late

scene in the cemetery where he 'confesses' his deceits to Brown,
and goes out of sight to vomit when Philipot tommy-guns
Concasseur, because he has never seen a man die before. He
takes on the role of commander with the same pleasure in a
game which he showed as a Victorian matron, and the men,
Philipot reports, believed in him. Jones's comic innocence is
reminiscent of Minty's in *England Made Me*: he too is ludicrous
and pathetic but never quite defeated. In the scene at Mère
Catherine's brothel where Jones amuses the girl Tin Tin,
humour is condemned by Concasseur, talking to Brown. 'You
have a sense of humour. I am in favour of jokes. They have a
political value. Jokes are a release for the cowardly and the
impotent' (1.5.3). In his Fascist view, that includes most people.
Jones makes jokes, in the setting of Duvalier's Haiti, not just a
release but a form of defiance and solidarity. Brown's narrative
begins with the thought that Jones deserves the modest
monument placed on the Haitian border more than generals or
politicians deserve their statues in public squares. His religion,
if any, is unknown, but the novel includes him in a funeral
Mass.

Although the Smiths' story is a subplot, they are the heart of
the novel. They might be called militant vegetarians, except
that they would dislike the adjective. Mr Smith stood as a
presidential candidate in his home state of Wisconsin in 1948,
on a vegetarian ticket. Because he looks and sounds so unlike a
politician, Brown thinks of him as 'the Presidential Candidate'
and inflates his status (as 'Truman's opponent') in the ignorant
minds of Haitian officials. The other great adventure in the
Smiths' lives was a holiday in Tennessee where they were
'freedom riders' in black-only buses; Mrs Smith was attacked
by racialists in Nashville. Racialism and all other human
failings, they believe, have a common origin in 'acidity' caused
by meat which, like alcohol, inflames 'the passions'. Such
crankiness would have been simply guyed in the earlier novels,
and it is a source of amusement in the early pages. They can
eat nothing the *Medea*'s restaurant provides, but they have
brought 'cartons and bottles' containing healthier foodstuffs:
Froment, Barmene, Yeastrol, Nuttoline and Slipper Elm Food.
'The captain gave a scared look at Mrs Smith's plate and cut
himself a wedge of duck.' (1.1.6) Struggling in the dark which
falls early on Port-au-Prince where the power is cut soon after

six, Mr Smith can still see: 'there's nothing like raw carrots for
the sight'. Offered eggs in the same evening, he admits, 'To tell
you the truth we are a little dogmatic about eggs' (1.2). Mr
Smith refers to vegetarianism as his 'King Charles's head'; on
the *Medea*, he is quaintly eccentric and Brown is tactfully
amused. In Haiti, both Smiths become astonishing.

The novel's foremost irony is that the Smiths have chosen
Haiti for a vegetarian centre overseas because they admire the
idea of a long-established black republic. Brown reads the
report Mr Smith writes, early in his visit, to his local newspaper
in Wisconsin:

> 'A black republic – and a black republic with a history, an
> art and a literature. It was as if I were watching the future of
> all the black African republics with their teething troubles
> over.' (He had no intention, I am sure, of appearing
> pessimistic.) (1.5.1)

A slave revolution in 1804 made Haiti independent of France
(although not of French culture), but its history has always
been violent and unhappy. The period of relative stability when
the Trianon flourished in the 1950s was a lull. Doctor Magiot
speaks realistically of 'my poor insignificant little Haiti' (3.4.4),
and explains to the Smiths that 'we live under the shadow of
your great and prosperous country' (2.1.5).

Brown shields his guests so far as he can from everyday life in
Port-au-Prince, so that there is irony in what they do not see.
Mr Smith has a letter of introduction to Doctor Philipot,
Secretary for Social Welfare, whom he hopes to interest in his
centre. Arriving at his hotel ahead of the Smiths, Brown finds
that Philipot, who has offended Duvalier, has cut his throat in
the empty swimming pool. Brown is sardonic: 'I didn't want
the Presidential Candidate to see a corpse coiled up under the
diving-board – not on his first night'. The lights are out when
the Smiths arrive, but they see what they take to be a beggar
asleep in the pool.

> 'The poor man. I've a good mind to take him down some
> money.'
> I was tempted to call up, 'Take him your letter of
> introduction. It's the Secretary for Social Welfare.' (1.2.1)

Flirting with Martha, Brown feels that 'the corpse in the pool seemed to turn our preoccupations into comedy . . . the corpse of Doctor Philipot belonged to a more tragic theme; we were only a sub-plot affording a little light relief' (1.2). The graver comedy which contrasts the Smiths' polite expectations with savage reality is not light relief, but the book's most earnest political point: that the liberal Middle America which the Smiths represent knows nothing about the outside world. When he hears that Jones has been arrested, Mr Smith, who is unafraid of 'any authorities', goes with Brown to ask the Secretary of State for Jones's release. He offers to stand bail. Brown explains to the Minister, who has never heard of bail, that it is a bribe, of two hundred dollars in Jones's case; speaking French because Smith does not understand it, they discuss how to make Jones presentable after the treatment he is certain to have undergone from the police (1.4.3). Smith refers to this meeting with warm praise for Haitian 'justice and respect for human dignity' when he reports it for the paper in Wisconsin.

There is irony too in what Mr Smith cannot or will not see. It is obvious to Brown, after their visit to the police cell, that Jones is a crook; Smith leaves with pride that 'we *are* involved' and 'I knew that he was thinking in the big terms I could not recognise, like Mankind, Justice, the Pursuit of Happiness' (1.4.4). Soon after Mr Smith has composed the report to Wisconsin, he and his wife are present when the Tontons interrupt Dr Philipot's funeral procession, smash the windows of the hearse, take away the coffin for obscure purposes connected with voodoo, and manhandle Mrs Smith when she tries to intervene. Mr Smith is shocked: 'he had loved people for their colour and he had been betrayed more deeply than those who hate' (1.5.1); he decides not to send the article. But he calls on Philipot's successor, who denies that any such incident has taken place, and Smith persists in his plan for a centre, ignoring the Secretary's obviously corrupt interest in vegetarian dollars. Taken out to see 'the new city' of Duvalierville, so far occupied by one beggar and one justice of the peace, he begins to have doubts about the regime's good intentions. When the Secretary explains how they can embezzle funds from the new centre, he at last despairs.

Reality touches him after he has passed the schoolchildren on their way to the cemetery where they are obliged to witness executions, on the Smiths' last evening in Port-au-Prince, and tears come to his eyes (2.1.2). His disillusion is moving to Brown, who respects his innocence for the same reason that Fowler feels grudging traces of respect for Pyle – because he despises his own cynicism. Greene seems divided between his sense of how dangerous Smith might be, unprotected by Brown or in a place where corruption was slightly better disguised, and admiration for his dedication, however misguided. The dark glasses of the Tontons are frequently contrasted with the clear blue gaze in the eyes of Mr Smith, which outstares Concasseur on one occasion, and reproaches Brown whenever he hints at faults in 'coloured people'. Smith is quixotic and like Quixote's his chivalrous interventions do more harm than good. The money he gives Duvalierville's beggar sets its justice of the peace in pursuit of him; on his last day he distributes dollars to the poor and fails to notice when the police 'close in on their prey', although Brown sees the facts of life, as 'men with two legs kick down men with one', 'men with two arms grasped those who were armless by their torsos and threw them to the ground'. This, incidentally, adds to the political theme that American aid is worse than useless. Mr Smith is comic at such moments, at an extreme point of comedy which is pathetic: 'I guess they won't squander that any worse than I would have done' (2.3.1). Brown calls him 'a saint' (2.3.1); the novel makes him a holy fool. There is little sign of his religious beliefs, but the Catholic in Brown implies that he is privileged by a special grace; remembering the prayer '*dona nobis pacem*', he reflects that Mr Smith was born with peace in his heart. He comes alive as a character because he divides his author's loyalties – away from the unseeing innocent but towards the committed failure. Smith is the stuff which saints are made of, and Greene has fallen in love with his character, in spite of himself.

It is often said that one of the hardest tasks in literature is to make a good character credible and attractive. *The Comedians* does so twice since Mrs Smith is worthy of her husband. The summit of Brown's tribute to Mr Smith is 'what an absurd fancy it had been for him to pose as a politician' (2.1.2). His wife is far more formidable and, as Brown thinks, would have made a better presidential candidate. Like her husband a pacifist on principle, she is a fighter by nature and willing to attack anyone, except Mr Smith. Dining with Dr. Magiot, Mr Smith observes that his wife once had a vegetarian bulldog.

> 'Of course it took some training.'
> 'It took authority', Mrs Smith said and her eyes challenged Doctor Magiot to deny it. (2.1.5)

Her relatively belligerent nature accords with Smith's mildness and with the gentle discipline of their life to produce moments of beautifully poised comedy: '"She has the heart of a tigress when roused", Mr Smith said, stirring the Yeastrol' (1.5.1). She shows her tiger's heart when Concasseur calls at the hotel early one morning to 'interrogate' Brown. Woken by the Tontons' rowdiness, Mrs Smith descends to his rescue. She has reached Chapter 4 of *Hugo's Self Taught*; her French, effective because crude, is made devastating by her fearless indignation.

> 'Hit him again,' Captain Concasseur told the man.
> '*Dégoutant*,' a voice said, '*Tout à fait dégoutant.*' (2.2.2)

One may feel sorry for the bulldog, but not for Concasseur. '*Montrez-moi votre warrant*' alarms him because he cannot understand the English word. She remembers the captain as the 'woman-striker' of Dr Philipot's funeral. When she threatens to bring her husband, the Tontons depart and she tends Brown with Listerine. The scene is just credible; surprise, force of personality, American French and the secret weapon of 'Presidential Candidate' – a joke of Brown's which Haiti takes seriously – assist her, as does the fact that under Duvalier not even a Tonton chief can be sure of himself. On the point of succumbing to the tragedy of Haiti, Brown is saved when life turns triumphantly comic, which is how he recalls it.

> I was as astonished as they were. The American accent with which the words were spoken had to me all the glow and vigour of Mrs Julia Ward Howe's *Battle Hymn of the Republic*. The grapes of wrath were trampled out in them and there was a flash of the terrible swift sword. They stopped my opponent with his fist raised to strike.

The rousing Battle Hymn expresses Brown's relief and helps

to make the victory seem convincing, however a Concasseur
would have behaved in real life. The careful syntax and
phrasing, and the pedantry which includes the full name and
title – one of many remnants of a Jesuit education – are
reminiscent of Fowler's patronising amusement at the vigorous,
unsophisticated American culture implied here by allusions to
the wording of the Battle Hymn. But Brown is a grateful ally;
some have seen the Smiths as Greene's apology for *The Quiet
American*. They assist his cause of persuading American readers
against Lyndon Johnson's type of anti-Communist foreign
policy. There is an unforeseen irony since America did come
humbly to terms with Papa Doc so soon after the novel was
written. But it is fitting that the Smiths should rescue Brown
again when he is a penniless refugee in Santo Domingo. The
Smiths deserve the term quixotic. They transcend their
absurdity, and in this scene quixotic innocence overcomes, for
once, the evil of Concasseur, and the experience of Brown – who
has often warned both Smiths against the danger of 'becoming
too involved'.

Greene's success with Brown's self-portrayal is crucial to the
novel's strength. 'Brown is not Greene' says the dedicatory
letter which prefaces the book. He has the moody intelligence
and sardonic humour to be found in the novels which are not
written in the first person. It may be a limitation in some
people's judgement of this phase in Greene's work, although it
is not a reasonable objection to *The Comedians*, that Brown is
akin to Fowler and Querry in tastes and outlook. This is
obviously a cast of mind with which Greene could comfortably
live during long periods of composition. Like Fowler and the
former Querry (and Plarr in *The Honorary Consul*), Brown is an
adulterous bachelor. Like them he is uneasy in religious
disbelief. Like them he is unduly severe in judging himself,
indeed contemptuous of his own best actions. Considered as a
version of a type interesting to Greene, Brown is the most fully
developed of all his variations on the themes of personality.

His relations with Martha have various comic and macabre
aspects. His rival is her suspicious son Angel (named perhaps
to lure critics who look for extraneous symbols) rather than her
husband Luis, who is possessive about everything in his
embassy except his wife. Their love-making is interrupted by
deaths – of the lover of Brown's mother, who died in bed with

him, and of Dr Philipot – and overshadowed by Brown's knowledge that her father was hanged in Germany for war crimes. He loves her for her 'goodness', saying that 'with goodness one can feel secure' (1.5.2). His insecurity is made very understandable in the *'curriculum vitae'* section which makes an excellent short story in itself. Fatherless and surrendered to the Jesuits at twelve by his adventurer (or 'comedian') mother, he has nowhere to think of as home – except the College of the Visitation which he thinks of very often. He feels no link with Monte Carlo, except that its casino started him on his chancy life.

> I felt a greater tie here, in the shabby land of terror, chosen for me by chance.
>   The first colours touched the garden, deep green and then deep red – transience was my pigmentation; my roots would never go deep enough anywhere to make me a home or make me secure with love. (3.1.2)

Greene can give a narrator such lines without making him sound, in context, mawkish or pretentious. Brown's empty, ruined Hotel Trianon (a name to speculate about, more than he does), during his last days there, is so well evoked that his twinges of self-pity are almost restrained. His literary manner, slightly precious here in taking pigmentation and roots from the colours in the garden, is just right for a well-educated hotelier. Passages of this kind give background to the irritability and jealousy of his affair with Martha. Jones has for a moment found a home, in her embassy, and Brown envies that.

She calls him a Berkleyan, one inclined to fantasise others or mentally colonise them (as Pyle does Fowler and Rycker Querry). His appreciation of the Smiths refutes her, and so does his observation of the minor characters: the integrity of the *Medea*'s captain, overwatched by his photograph of a stern Dutch wife; the relish for voodoo in Joseph whom Brown values for his skill with rum-punches; the comical 'innocence' of Philipot's obsession with owning a Bren; ironic knowingness in the Syrian trader Hamit – 'He knew as many intimate things as a prostitute's dog' (1.5.2). He admits to being baffled by the complacent Luis. His memories of Martha do not bring her to life. Greene would say that at least one lifeless character is necessary, especially in a novel of such amplitude as *The Comedians*. She assists the plot, furthers the theme that Europeans are farcical in contrast to Haitians, and brings out facets of Brown's unhappiness, but she is dull. Envious of his Catholic background, she calls herself 'a Protestant nothing' (3.2.1) and this leads her to an interesting verdict on her lover whom she calls a *prêtre manqué* – a better term than 'spoiled priest' (3.2.1).

Brown is more skilled in friendship than in love. His point of view lends saintliness to Mr Smith and stature to Doctor Magiot, both of whom he makes father-figures, and he finally sees an unlikely brother in Jones, fatherless and rootless too. Magiot illustrates the difficulty of creating a good man in fiction. Brown tells us about the doctor's size, strength, gentleness, medical and practical skills, presence (like a Roman emperor's), and grave good manners (reminiscent to Brown of the nineteenth century); dozens of other terms of praise would fit. He is a necessary hero in a novelist who is normally suspicious of conventional heroism and more creative in showing virtue in a Minty, a whisky-priest, a burnt-out case, or a Jones. Magiot cannot compare with them in giving the illusion of life. Greene could not risk making Magiot more true because less good. His solid worth corrects the impression that all educated Haitians are criminal or unstable, and emphasises the theme that automatic anti-Communism is not the best policy for the United States when Papa Doc has him murdered by Tontons at the end in politeness to the Americans who are soon to re-establish diplomatic relations. Magiot's Communism is undoctrinaire and even sceptical about Cuba; a political stance which pleases Greene but also suits his thesis. The Smiths are so much larger than their roles that they make him seem contrived. His gravity is most vivid when touched by humour – 'I wouldn't settle in Duvalierville if I were you. It is not the right *ambiance* for vegetarianism' (2.1.5) – or by the romantic innocence which admires Brown's mother for her French Resistance medal which her son suspects is a theft or a lover's memento. It is tempting to surmise that the 'innocence' in Greene's adverse sense would lie much deeper in such a man than the novel is willing to go. His effectiveness as a good man owes most to the vividness of the corrupt and vicious politicians and Tontons. They create a demand in the reader for his sober sense which comes as a relief. He reassures, perhaps, in the way of dull but worthy successors – Richmond, Edgar, Malcolm – in Shakespearean tragedies, although he is not to succeed the other 'father-doctor' who stays all through the novel concealed in his palace. More even than Martha's, his role demonstrates Brown's insecurity and longing for the goodness with which one feels secure.

It is an old boast in the Society of Jesus that, given a child, they can answer for the man. Brown is a study of how the Jesuits' hold remains in a *Catholique non croyant* who – in the opposite case to Greene's – was trained in childhood and youth as a promising candidate for the priesthood. The Fathers of the Visitation 'half-expected' a vocation in the young Brown, who was more excited by faith than by sex, during adolescence; and although he shrugs off Martha's *'prêtre manqué'* with affected incomprehension, he constantly thinks of the Fathers. His memories are unmarked by the resentment with which Greene's characters usually remember school. The novel closes with grim thoughts that, while his life might have been different, Brown is lost in the flat plain of uninvolvement, away from the 'heights' and 'abysses' of life. Regret for what was lost when he 'left involvement behind . . . in the College of the Visitation' haunts the narrative. Reluctantly attending a voodoo ceremony, Brown is offended by the blasphemy of its borrowings from Catholic liturgy, and angry when he sees Philipot among the initiates: 'he had been educated like myself by the Jesuits; he had attended the Sorbonne' (2.2.1). After so many references to the fact, the needlessness of 'like myself' implies that he feels a personal affront in Philipot's apostasy. At other times he sounds bitter or indignant about other people's lapses from Catholic standards, especially those of reason. Luis too went to school with the Jesuits and Brown tells Martha, 'They taught us to reason so that at least we know the kind of part we play now' (2.1.2) – a distinct claim, with an almost melodramatic note, to be as an ex-Catholic superior to other comedians. When Philipot proposes that help from the gods of Dahomey, who participate in voodoo, is needed against Papa Doc, Brown protests, 'You are a Catholic. You believe in reason' (2.1.4). At such moments Brown loses his pose of a cynical onlooker at life.

Regret for lost faith appears more obviously, mistakenly perhaps given the art which presents it in his waking mind, in Brown's subconscious. Greene believes in dreams but rarely finds creative use for them. In the first paragraph of Part Three Brown dreams that he is a boy at the communion rail in the school chapel and that the priest gives bourbon biscuits (Angel's favourites) to everyone else, leaving him sullen, in an aisle turned into an aviary of parrots. This kind of alienation, crude in itself, takes on life in relation to Brown's brooding about his homelessness. His roots are in the school chapel, and he is imperfectly deracinated.

Wondering about his 'never quiet conscience', Brown speaks predictably about having been 'injected' with conscience, 'without my consent, when I was too young to know, by the Fathers of the Visitation' (3.4.3). This is self-denigration rather than a serious objection by someone who has been taught to reason. Struggling to save Mr Smith from a horde of mutilated beggars in the Post Office, he touches 'a stiff inhuman stump':

> I forced it on one side, and I felt revolted by myself, as though I were rejecting misery. The thought even came to me, What would the Fathers of the Visitation have said to me? (2.1.1)

Brown's good nature appears in his protection of the Smiths, in the risks he takes to smuggle Jones into asylum, in his driving Joseph to the voodoo ceremony, knowing that Joseph will otherwise try to limp there, and in small actions such as stirring a Tonton sentry in danger of being found asleep on duty – 'I might as well do someone a good turn' (1.5.4). He is obliged to choose his side in his dealings with Captain Concasseur (one of the best-named characters in Greene). They notice each other with mutual dislike at the police station where Mr Smith outstares the captain, and exchange threats at Dr Philipot's aborted funeral. At Mère Catherine's, where they clash for the first time, Brown shows a commitment which Concasseur recognises:

> 'A capitalist will always be loyal if he is allowed his cut of twenty-five per cent.'
> 'A little humanity is necessary too.'
> 'You speak like a Catholic.'
> 'Yes. Perhaps. A Catholic who has lost his faith.' (1.5.3)

This scene makes it plain that Concassuer could kill Brown with impunity and might do so at whim. Concasseur later offers to be 'friends' if Brown will lure Jones out of the embassy; the alternative seems to be 'interrogation' of the kind Joseph suffered. Although Brown wants to be rid of Jones, he does not consider that working with Concasseur is the only safe way to achieve that and the only way to keep his hotel. A business-man who really saw life as God's practical joke would collaborate with the Tontons, for twenty-five per cent.

Brown's integrity at such moments counts for more than his habitual reflections about how cynical he is. But integrity achieves next to nothing in *The Comedians*. Magiot's farewell letter tells Brown that Catholicism has given him a humanist faith akin to the doctor's own sceptical Communism; this kind of faith seems an ultimate defence against nihilism rather than a positive force for good. Magiot knows when he writes the letter that the Tontons are about to kill him. Philipot, the other leader of Haitian resistance, is last seen in defeat, consoled only by his naïve admiration for Jones: 'I would like to write about him to the Queen of England' (3.4.3). The novel makes evil seem strong and natural; resistance is usually comical, pathetic and dignified by frailty rather than heroism. Mrs Smith rejects the term 'heroic' when Brown tries to praise her. She speaks of her husband's political campaign as a 'gesture'. Gestures of dissent are all that is possible in Greene's 'nightmare republic'. When Concasseur tells Mère Catherine not to waste Seven-Up on Brown, she brings him another rum, still mixed with Seven-Up. He comments 'She was a brave woman' (1.5.3). But her gesture, Brown's rejection of Concasseur, Jones's and Philipot's war-plans and Magiot's letter are far from being signs of future victory; they are in the spirit of the novel because they are almost hopeless.

On the voyage back to Haiti, in the early pages, Brown thinks that God's purpose may be 'an extreme point of comedy'. We reach such a point when Mr Smith talks earnestly with Papa Doc's ludicrous and ghastly officials, or when Philipot praises Jones. Only Petit Pierre's 'laughter of despair' would be possible there. The evil of Concasseur, like the goodness of the Smiths, quells comedy, and so does death. Brown says of the dead that 'they rebuked our levity' (3.4.4). A painting which he contemplates in the empty Trianon does the same. Showing dancers in bright masks at a carnival, at first it gives 'an impression of gaiety'; on closer inspection one sees the ugliness of the masks and, at the centre of the dance, 'a cadaver in grave-clothes' (3.3.1). This passage is as good a guide to the novel as Magiot's letter. Look more closely, the novel affirms, and gaiety fades.

The painting recalls many other contrasts of light and darkness. The Haitians fear that the Tontons' dark glasses hide the eyes of zombies. After dusk, only the Tontons use the roads because everyone else is afraid of the graveyard spectre, Baron Samedi, a second nickname now for Papa Doc; before he came to power, dancers in the Baron's costume used to stage a comic turn for tourists on hotel terraces. The vivid tropical colours of the landscape give an illusion of gaiety which is always liable to be cancelled, as it is when a passing Tonton limousine showers dust over the bright scene Brown is admiring on the trip to Duvalierville (2.1.3). Comedy in the spirit of Brown's mother, who lived for 'fun', is reproached by death, and the comedians' antics are often interrupted by death. Jokes about death turn sour. Brown is searching for a favourite paperweight – for letters which are not urgent – marked R.I.P., when he finds Doctor Philipot's corpse. The novel concludes, appropriately, with Brown's first day in his new job as an undertaker's assistant. Images which may be remembered when Brown's reflections on comedy and tragedy are forgotten give force to the novel's theme, that life is a comedy at which the angels might weep: the undertaker twins sitting on the terrace of the Trianon, eating icecreams with Doctor Philipot's little son, while the Tontons smash his hearse on the road below; Mr Smith wallowing innocently in the swimming-pool cleansed of Dr Philipot's blood; the one completed building at Duvalierville, which Mr Smith takes to be a Greek theatre, an arena for cockfights.

Querry's dying words, 'It's absurd, or else' summarise the meaning of *The Comedians*. Its message, that the United States should not support Duvalier, is completed in Brown's interview for a job with an American company in the Dominican Republic, whose humourless manager (a Coca-Cola drinker) is completely unaware of what is happening over the border and decides that Brown's flight means that he is a Communist. The meaning concludes on the last page, in a dream in which Jones tells Brown that he is dying because death is 'in his part' but that he has 'one good line' which makes everyone laugh 'till the tears come': 'This is a good place'. The place is not just Haiti, which suits Greene the novelist as well as Greene the journalist committed to a message for America. Brown thinks about the painting of the masquers, that wherever it hung 'Baron Samedi would be walking in the nearest graveyard even though the graveyard was in Tooting Bec'. Brooding on the fact of Martha's father's war-crimes, he decides that: 'Haiti was not an exception in a sane world: it was a small slice of everyday taken at random. Baron Samedi walked in all our graveyards' (1.5.2). If that means that the world is absurd, and evil in Haiti only less disguised than in Tooting Bec, the message is perhaps weakened by the meaning. But Brown knows at the end, though he believes in nothing, that life is unbearable without a faith, however desperate; and that is the novel's assertion.

The most interesting kind of tragi-comedy in all Greene's work appears in the story of Father León Rivas in *The Honorary Consul* (1973). Knowing the worst about politics and religion as priest of a *barrio*, or poor district, in Paraguay, he lives with two desperate, incompatible faiths. Unwilling to preach the virtues of poverty to parishioners even poorer than he is, or to serve Mass before people who cannot afford to drink wine, he has become a '*politico*'. Suspended from his 'faculties' as a priest, he has married himself to a simple, pious girl called Marta, and he now leads a terrorist gang which has crossed into northern Argentina planning to kidnap the American ambassador and 'exchange' him for political prisoners in Paraguay. He is in deadly earnest. 'I will not listen to you if you joke' he says to his prisoner (3.3). But his predicament as priest-guerrilla is somewhat ridiculous, because he has bungled the kidnapping and caught a nonentity, Charley Fortnum, drunken British honorary consul in a small provincial town. Although León is a comic figure, the comedy does not demean him. As a half-lapsed priest and an inefficient, intellectual, left-wing insurgent, he combines two roles Greene had used before. Their conflict in León creates an original character whose stance of baffled idealism in hopeless circumstances is a fine expression of 'the

trag-comic region of La Mancha' – the imaginative world of
Greene's mature work.

The Honorary Consul has a central stage, in the hut where the
consul is held, and Greene has commented on this as the
'logical conclusion' of an impulse in all his novels to 'escape the
vast liquidity of the novel' and direct the characters as though
in a play. 'Almost the whole story', he says, 'is contained in the
hut.'[87] Many scenes are set elsewhere, but the conversations in
the hut dramatise the ironic centre of the novel with delicate
strength:

> 'These things are a bit above my head, Father', Charley
> Fortnum said, lying propped on his elbow on the coffin and
> looking down at the dark head which still showed the faint
> trace of a tonsure through the hair, like a prehistoric camp in
> a field seen from a plane. He interjected 'Father' as often as
> he could: it was somehow reassuring. A father didn't usually
> kill his son, although of course it had been a near thing in the
> case of Abraham. 'I am not to blame, Father.'
> 'I am not blaming you, Señor Fortnum, God Forbid.'
> 'I can see how the American Ambassador from your point
> of view – well he was a legitimate objective. But me – I'm not
> even a proper Consul and the English are not in this fight,
> Father.'
> The priest muttered a cliché absent-mindedly, 'They say
> one man has to die for the people.'
> 'But that was what the crucifiers said, not the Christians.'
> The priest looked up. 'Yes, you are right,' he said, 'I was
> not thinking when I spoke. You know your Testament.'
> 'I have not read it since I was a boy. But that's the kind of
> scene which sticks in the mind. Like Struwwelpeter.'
> 'Struwwelpeter?'
> 'He had his thumbs cut off.'
> 'I never heard of him. Is he one of your martyrs?'
> 'No, no, it's a nursery story, Father.'
> 'Have you children?' the priest asked sharply.
> 'No, but I told you. In a few months there should be one
> around . . .' (3.3)

The novel is so closely constructed that commentary on a
passage of this length involves everything else.

'A bit above my head' catches Charley's tone, slangy, modest and apologetic, but his memory of John 18.14, where the Jews consider that 'it is expedient that one man should die for the people', and his quirkish association of Christ with Straw Peter, are typical of the way his commonplace mind has an unpredictable quality. Like the Smiths of *The Comedians* he begins as a caricature and develops in human interest. As a whisky-consul, solemnly discoursing on 'the proper measure', 'boasting about his jeep "Fortnum's Pride"', recalling schooldays when he was 'Fortnum and Mason', and explaining his 'respect' for his girl at Señora Sanchez's brothel, he is a familiar comic type, sympathetic in Greene's world because an undefeated failure. His pronouncements have an individual flavour: 'Nationality's thicker than water, though that's a nasty term, when you think of it'; 'thicker' is partly explained by his reference to syrup of figs, suffered in childhood; 'if you conquer fear', he proposes, 'you conquer your human nature, too' because 'it's a bit like the balance of nature' and he goes on to talk about spiders and flies (2.1). Greene is more inventive and persuasive with Charley than with Jones in *The Comedians*, perhaps because the consul is so transparent a failure. 'I've sat on worse things', he says when drunk on the floor of the Italian Club, 'including horses' (2.1). His hatred of horses, which dates from childhood riding-lessons, contrasts with the 'machismo' of traditional Argentine lore, celebrated by the novelist Doctor Saavedra (a minor character whose absurdities have been described above in Chapter 1, pp. 18–19). Greene's novel is written with disdain for 'machismo', the Latin American cult of masculine pride in courage and virility. Charley is one of its alternative types of hero.

León as a terrorist resembles Mr Smith as a presidential candidate; his meekness, like Smith's, appears in the contrast with the role for which he is absurdly miscast. His courtesy to 'Señor Fortnum' accords with his concern for Charley's well-being. The ground is damp, he explains a little later in this scene, and they have provided the coffin to guard against rheumatism. There was no thought of the coffin being 'handy later on'; in the *barrio* there is far more demand for coffins than for beds. To have bought a bed would have caused comment. The complete absence of any sense of irony in León's explanation of the coffin reminds us of the social background which is too poor to indulge in ironic amusement, but there is minimised comedy in the first sentence of this extract, where 'propped on his elbow' pretends to ignore the unusual nature of the prop and its point as a *memento mori* for the consul and his captors.

The image which follows is equally well suited to the incongruities of the situation and to the presentation of León. It is diverting in the number of its odd comparisons: not only the priest's hair and the field of grass, the tonsure and the camp, but also the two scales of observation, since the plane's height makes the camp visible while proximity reveals the tonsure, and two time scales since the camp is old and the tonsure recent. We may reflect that while the camp is dead, the priesthood denoted by the tonsure is not quite extinct in León; and that while the camp is of academic interest the vestige of tonsure implies, with an intimacy which makes León seem vulnerable, what he has lost and the awkwardness of his present position.

There is a willingness to confide, in Charley's memory of a children's book (Heinrich Hoffmann's *Struwwelpeter*), and in León's lapse into curiosity about martyrs, which is characteristic of their strange relations. An odd formality on both sides adds to the comedy below the surface of the dialogue: Charley concedes the other's point of view where an American ambassador is concerned; León concedes his misappropriation of Scripture and pays a priestly-sounding compliment. The tone of their conversation here belongs to a more normal context – a British Council reception, perhaps. Such urbanity adds to the dramatic interest in whether León could become a killer. Political creeds in this century, like religious beliefs in earlier times, have caused polite people to act ruthlessly – perhaps the disciplines of the priesthood have equipped León as a militant of the Left. In the witty observation that saints' lives and old fashioned nursery-books have horrors in common lies the thought that kidnappers resort to the same sort of brutality. But León sounds too thoughtful and hesistant to be one of life's victimisers. We are told elsewhere that 'he had the patience of someone who was more used to enduring pain than inflicting it' (3.3). This is established by his behaviour and his talk throughout the novel. He has the air of being a failure in a good cause which is redeeming in Greene. His gentleness is very convincing when he brings in the whisky Charley has ordered from town and carefully counts the change, offering a friendly warning when he sees how fast the level goes down in the bottle. Successful terrorism should be made of sterner stuff. His deputy Aquino has been toughened by torture in police cells but he too seems out of his element as he grumbles about the consul's needs – 'this is not a hotel, Charley' – while attending to them; and he quotes the poems he wrote in captivity. León's 'wife' is pathetically proud to be a priest's 'woman' – they argue her status, without rancour – and Pablo, another member of the group, is prone to tears. Doctor Plarr, called in when Aquino shoots Charley in the ankle to stop him escaping, is the novel's chief observer of events. Ironically contemplating 'the desperados', he prays 'For heaven's sake let this comedy end in comedy. None of us are suited to tragedy' (5.3).

The menace of tragedy touches the comedy of this scene between Charley and León, and much of the rest of the novel. Misremembering the Gospel, León discovers a Marxist precept. Aquino will argue that if the terms are not met, Charley must be killed for the sake of the next attempt to further the people's cause. Circumstances have half-converted León to this principle, but he readily accepts Charley's correction based on the opposite Christian principle which sides with any victim. This lies at the heart of the problem for South American Catholics, living under repressive government in poor countries and wishing to support resistance movements. Nobody in this novel is portentous about the theme of Catholic or Communist commitment (as Doctor Magiot is, on occasions, in *The Comedians*). The truth, several characters observe, is elusive. Doctor Humphries, an English teacher, finds that truth is 'like a difficult sentence which his pupils never succeeded in getting grammatically right' (4.2). He remarks that 'contrary to common belief the truth is nearly always funny' but adds that he does not want the truth about himself because 'it's always other people who are funny' (1.1). Minor characters who are innocent or indifferent do not want to know the truth about themselves. These include Plarr's mother who lives alone in Buenos Aires comforting herself with creamcakes and the attentions of sycophantic priests; Sir Henry Belfrage, the British ambassador, almost as complacent although more kindly viewed, who complains about American imperialism when his breakfast eggs are fried on both sides; the American ambassador, who appears only in Sir Henry's aggrieved thoughts about him, a teetotaller who serves bad wine. Neither diplomat is concerned about Fortnum's fate – or about the social and political circumstances which provoke the kidnappings. The American refuses to believe that he was the intended victim. Doctor Saavedra, who declines to sign Plarr's letter to *The Times* which appeals on Charley's behalf, because he finds the prose style unsatisfactory, is a figure of fun cut off by his devotion to machismo from the real life of Argentina.[88] He gains in dignity, however, when Plarr discovers his poverty and 'the hunger of his literary obsession' (4.2).

Truth perplexes most of the other characters in various ways. The exception is Colonel Perez, with Hartep and Vigot among the most vivid of Greene's policemen, who has no doubt of his ability to detect the truth and to misrepresent it in the interests of order, and his career. Latin cultural assumptions sometimes deflect his judgement. He decides that Plarr cannot be involved in Charley's kidnapping when he learns that the consul's wife is the doctor's mistress: a husband is necessary to an affair. Travelling in an aeroplane with Plarr, he speaks sceptically about a rumour that the Virgin has defused a bomb placed in a church. Plarr tells him that further inquiry is needed since 'a miracle is very much like a crime' (4.1). When Perez replies that he thinks the plane's engines are keeping it in the sky, not 'divine intervention', the plane dips in an air-pocket and the policeman looks 'uneasy'. These are moments of light relief, however. In the last stages of the story, Perez very competently imposes his own version of Charley's rescue on the world, laying all the blame on the 'fanatic priest' (5.5).

Relations between husband and wife or lover and mistress are less interesting in Greene than relations between rivals: Bendrix and Henry, Fowler and Pyle, Querry and Rycker; more might have been made of Brown's dealings with Martha's husband than is made of his affair with her. Charley Fortnum and Eduardo Plarr are ingeniously matched rivals. Neither is a religious believer; both are apolitical; but they both become 'involved'. Worldly judges consider Plarr a failure as a doctor because he practises among the provincial poor when he might have made a career in Buenos Aires. He does so out of loyalty to his English, liberal father whom he last saw when he was fourteen and who has since then been a political prisoner across the river in Paraguay. This bond commits him, more than half against his will, to helping his old schoolfriend León in the hope that his father may be among the prisoners released if the kidnappers succeed. Meanwhile his labours in the *barrio* make him a 'serious' character in the sense in which Charley is not. A maté farmer, Charley was made honorary consul by an over-indulgent ambassador, when he took some 'minor royals' on a successful picnic. He finds it hard to persuade his kidnappers that an honorary consul is not a 'proper', salaried diplomat but a person of very small official consequence. He is not entitled to the flag and 'CC' plates on his car, or strictly, to the Cadillac imported every two years which makes the position financially worth his while. As a whisky-consul, whom the embassy finds an embarrassment, he is presumably the least valuable hostage with any claim to diplomatic status in all South America. A further disqualification, in the conventional view of Doctor Humphries, is that he has recently made an 'unsuitable' marriage, to the girl Clara – forty years his junior – from Señora Sanchez's. A familiar comic type, sympathetic in Greene's world because an undefeated failure, he develops in interest and sympathy as a quixotic lover.

Clara does not marry for love. She misses the companionship of the girls, though not the men, when she leaves the brothel and she finds marriage bewildering, like 'another girl's dress'. She becomes Eduardo's mistress when he gives her a pair of sunglasses; it is her habit to comply. He suffers from a kind of sexual ennui; he cannot fall in love and he has become bored with women's bodies too well-known to him since Argentine medical ethics are very lax. He thinks of Clara as an 'obsession' in which deceiving Charley has a part. She becomes pregnant, and Charley is glad that 'Ted' is looking after her. This obvious irony is sustained throughout the period when, as Charley's fellow prisoner, Eduardo is obliged to listen sympathetically to the anxious husband's fretting about 'the little bastard' – Charley's affectionate term for his child to be – and gratitude for the doctor's friendship with his wife. The pressure on Eduardo is more intense because he cannot understand his 'obsession'. His 'savage desire' to tell Charley the truth is checked only by professional concern for his patient's physical injury (5.1). The reader senses the deeper irony, that Eduardo is jealous of

Charley's love. León points this out to him just at the moment
when, raising his voice in argument, Eduardo betrays the truth
about the little bastard's fatherhood. In the quarrel which
follows, the doctor pleads that the child is as much an accident
as the kidnapping; and he comes to the suspicion of God which
has occurred to Brown, that there must be 'a great joker
somewhere who likes to give a twist to things'. He acknowledges
that he is jealous of Charley, which he thinks 'another comic
twist'. These passages explore an observation of Colonel Perez's,
that it is usually a friend whom one betrays; Charley comes to
terms with the betrayal when, facing death, he recognises
another twist in the fact that there is no other friend to whom
he can trust his wife and child. It is Eduardo who dies, for
Colonel Perez is much more efficient than the desperados;
reunited with Clara, Charley decides that the boy they expect
should be named after his father, because 'I loved Eduardo in a
way' (5.5). 'Poor drunken Charley Fortnum wins the game',
the doctor says, shortly before he goes out to his death.
Charley's is an attractively charitable victory, and his story has
a sort of happy ending.

'Father' is one of the novel's key words. Unable after so long
to picture his father who, he learns, has died in captivity,
Eduardo finds himself borrowing the features of Charley
Fortnum, yet another twist of irony. Charley is haunted by
unhappy memories of his father who made him take the riding-
lessons, which he still resents. But understanding now why it
was that his father drank, he begins to feel sympathy. Charley
coaxes Father Rivas with his title, at first from policy since 'a
father didn't usually kill his son', but gradually from appreciation
of León's unmistakable priestly charisma. The other kidnappers
including León's 'wife' call him 'Father' without irony. The
scene in which he is recognised by an old blind man, who
wants a 'good', poor man's Father to anoint his dead wife,
connects the point that he cannot rid himself of his priesthood
with his role as a quixotic champion of the poor: 'I want the
Father to say the Mass. I do not want the Archbishop's priest' –
he hears 'a priest's voice'. The novel refers to 'Father Rivas'
except when adopting the point of view of Aquino or Eduardo
who knew him as a boy. This seems increasingly appropriate as
the group of Catholic characters, approaching the new 'deadline'
which Colonel Perez sets once his paras are in position,

contemplate the likelihood of death and look to 'the Father' rather than the chief. Martha persuades León to say Mass and he does so, interrupted by the Colonel from outside.

> *'Ite Missa est.'*
> The voice on the loudspeaker answered like a liturgical response, 'You have fifteen minutes left.' (5.4)

Taken out of context, this may seem self-parody, because it so boldly unites Greene as 'religious' novelist and author of thrillers. The union works brilliantly in the pages which lead up to the deaths of León and Eduardo, the excitement of approaching action tingeing our sense of León's conflict of duties. He is almost completely the priest when he humbly urges Charley to confess – a scene held just on the edge of comedy without quite becoming funny. Charley feels sorry for the Father and discovers forgiveness of his own father: 'Poor bugger, he thought'. Yet León's integrity makes it seem still possible that he will act as the terrorist sooner than let Aquino, who is resolved on a revolutionary execution, take the responsibility and the sin. When Eduardo goes out to try to parley with Perez and is shot down, León follows and dies near him, grateful that he has been spared from murder. He begins to confess and Eduardo attempts a joke, saying 'Ego te absolvo' but is too tired to laugh aloud. The Catholic reader may be reminded of modern views on the nature of the comic which suggest that the most extreme point of comedy is not tragic but religious. Any reader may respond to the peculiar *frisson* Greene can give, by the contexts which he creates for them, to the great formulae of his religion.

5

Entertainments

The distinction which Greene implies by calling some of his novels 'entertainments' is explained in many of his reviews and critical essays. 'Journey into Success' (1952), an article on A. E. W. Mason, asks why some able popular novelists do not 'progress' beyond detective stories and historical adventures: 'Why didn't they grow, with such a technical start – well, a little more worthy of consideration?'[89] Mason's fault is said to be detachment. He had no 'allegiances'; he 'never surrendered himself'. Greene names Conrad, by contrast, as a serious artist, and concludes: 'They had set themselves different summits.' He began his career with the highest summits in view; James, Ford, Conrad. In *Stamboul Train* Mr Savory caricatures the popular novelist without allegiances and Greene's other thrillers of the 1930s, *A Gun for Sale* (1936) and *The Confidential Agent*, were, he says, means of financing the more ambitious books which, before the war, sold poorly.[90] Mr Savory would stress that all good novels are entertainments; and he would presumably agree with the critic who wrote of Greene that 'the most serious thing he or any novelist can give his readers is not religious revelation or social truth, but stories and still more stories'.[91] Greene would be suspicious of the principle of stories for their own sake. Working at the craft gives force to the story, but the creative novelist who grows up, he maintains, is involved in life, which brings religious and social allegiances. Where these are less marked and the thrills or amusements of the story make lighter demands on our consideration, Greene would say, an entertainment is to be distinguished from a serious novel.

He gave some of his early 'entertainments' less attention. He wrote *The Confidential Agent* in three weeks, stimulated by

114

benzedrine, while composing *The Power and the Glory* much more slowly.[92] Although there is no question which novel is more worthy of consideration, there are obvious connections between the narrative gifts and allegiances which survived the benzedrine and those of the serious novels. Whatever Greene says, his work has always repudiated the idea of a strict separation between literary art and vulgar entertainment. *Stamboul Train* was written to make money quickly but it is the first novel in which he successfully illustrates the perception of life which made him a creative writer. He was influenced as much by the instinct for story-telling which links Stevenson with Buchan and Mason as by the higher allegiances which Stevenson the artist shares with James and Conrad; and practice in writing thrillers, where the story matters most, helped to develop the peculiar art of his best books.

There are passages in *A Gun for Sale* which are written in the anonymous, group-style of any modern adventure story.

> It hadn't been a satisfactory job; what had begun as a plain robbery had ended with two murders and the death of the murderer. There was a mystery about the whole affair; everything hadn't come out. Mather was up there on the top floor now with the head of the political department; they were going through Sir Marcus' private papers. It really seemed as if the girl's story might be true. (8.2)

These are a policeman's thoughts; his phrasing could belong to any writer's policeman. Escalation of a mystery, in this case from a stolen banknote to murder, political assassination and international crisis, is a convention. Sir Marcus is – with a hint of the foreign in *cus* – the right name for a magnate whose papers will reveal skulduggery on an international scale. Sir Mark would be too respectable. 'It *really* seemed' tells us how astonishing everything will be when it comes out; 'the girl' has been mixed up in an extraordinary affair; 'the head of the political department' sounds impressive, and 'going through' the private papers sounds more exciting than 'reading' them. 'Heavens, Mather, look at this!' The style translates easily into routines of screen entertainment.

John Buchan invented the simplified story of crime, espionage and pursuit involving ordinary people, although his people

were gentlemen: Richard Hannay, Sandy Arbuthnot, Edward
Leithen. Greene's review of Buchan's last novel observes that
The Thirty-nine Steps (1914) has been 'a pattern for adventure-
writers ever since' and asks 'who will forget the thrill in 1916
. . . as the hunted Leithen [in *The Power House*] "ran like a thief
in a London thoroughfare on a June afternoon"?'[93] Greene's
plot devices are Buchan's: how to get out of London without
money; how to evade the police when they will not believe your
story; how to prevent, in the next few hours of hide-and-seek, a
world war. But when he mentions Buchan's influence on *A Gun
for Sale*, he qualifies it: by the 1930s, 'it was no longer a Buchan
world' because the First World War and the Depression had
discredited Buchan's patriotic upper-class heroes.[94] His thrillers
drew on lower social strata; the 'hero' of *A Gun for Sale* comes
from the meanest imaginable social depth.

Very conservative in conventions, thrillers are often, like
Buchan's, politically conservative in their assumptions. Greene's
are not. The capitalist Sir Marcus is the villain of *A Gun for Sale*
and his killing, watched with satisfaction by his valet, seems an
act of justice or, at least, of appropriate revenge. Greene dislikes
and disclaims symbols, but a socialist reader in 1936 might well
have seen this character's extreme old age and physical frailty,
wheelchair and hoarse whisper, as signs of the current state of
capitalism. The title refers to the profits to be made in dealings
in metals for arms, from which Sir Marcus profits, as well as to
the hired gunman, Raven, whom he employs to kill a foreign
statesman and start a lucrative war; its point was missed in the
United States where Doubleday changed the title to *This Gun
for Hire*. Money and violence are frequently associated: a
journalist predicting war (in 1.5) urges colleagues to buy
armament shares and make a fortune. Greene's essay 'At Home'
(1940) expresses a leading idea of his early novels, and especially
of the thrillers.

> Violence comes to us more easily because it was so long
> expected – not only by the political sense but also by the
> moral sense. The world we lived in could not have ended any
> other way.[95]

A political and moral outlook appears in many of the novel's
pictures of poverty subject to brash inhuman commerce: the

attendant in a magazine shop in Soho sits, 'a parody of a woman, dirty and depraved, crouched under the most lovely figures, the most beautiful vacant faces the smut photographers could hire' (2.10). Nottwich is poor with a northern English frankness which the novel approves: 'there was no excuse in Nottwich for one half of the world being ignorant of how the other half lived' (7.1). More dreadful than its slums, moreover, are the new estates of redbrick, gabled houses, advertised as 'Cozyholmes', which speculative builders are offering on hire-purchase; they represent – worse than poverty – 'the meanness of the spirit' (2.3). It seems ironically fitting that the killer Raven should bring his hostage Anne to such a house, 'Sleepy Nuik'. Its petit-bourgeois meanness returns to mind when women fight and squabble for bargains at a jumble sale. The policeman Mather notices a 'hard driven face' and a head which ducks as if expecting a blow but comes up again 'with a sour unconquerable malice' (3.3). England has made most of the book's people this way. At the highest and lowest extremes of society, violence is undisguised. Sir Marcus's agent explains to Raven, whose gun he has bought:

> 'My clients are really quite the best people. The acts of violence – they regard them as war.'
> 'And I and the old man . . .' Raven said.
> 'Are in the front trench.' (1.3)

This world, the novel says, can only end one way.

It is very effective in this kind of gloomy apprehension. Raven is a more credible hired assassin than his glamorous counterparts in more romantic stories. Thin, ugly, hare-lipped, he is obsessed with his gun as a compensation for physical and psychological disabilities – these more crudely presented than those of Pinkie, for whom he is a trial model. In action he is a mixture of naïveté and cunning. He accepts payment in five-pound notes in numbered sequence, but he succeeds in evading the police long enough to track down and kill the double-dealing Sir Marcus, aided by chance only as much as a thriller allows. His role in a Buchan novel would be that of a man falsely suspected, hunted by the police while hunting an enemy in order to prove his innocence. Anne Crowder, the good-natured chorus girl whom he takes prisoner and who befriends him, takes this role and is suspected by her fiancé Mather. Raven is guilty (his name chosen for the colour), although his murders are understandable given his appalling childhood, which helps to explain Anne's sympathy. His cantankerous thoughts about Christianity, and evident need to 'confess' when trusted by Anne, indicate the possibility of his salvation but the last words of the sentence in which he dies apparently send him to hell. In this respect the book seems muddled, and outside the scope of an entertainment.

It is very successful with minor characters: grotesques such as the unfrocked parson Acky and his equally crazed wife, united in an inexplicable love; the pathetic Chief Constable who longs for another war in which to bully conscientious objectors; the sybarite Davis, who ogles chorus girls and slakes his lust with icecream and coffee; and the medical student Buddy – a remarkable miniature satire inspired by hatred of another English type of arrested development. These figures verge on comedy, too horrifying and convincing to be funny, while we can see how a little more detachment or indulgence might make them so.

The Confidential Agent and *The Ministry of Fear* (1943) develop the idea that war does not so much change society as bring into the open conditions which peacetime disguises. The Confidential Agent, called D., comes from an equally anonymous country (which we take to be Spain) torn apart by civil war and is impressed at first by the calm and security of England. He is soon disillusioned. What he glimpses of the life of a fourteen-year-old maid at his boarding house persuades him that 'barbarity' is preferable to the civilisation of prosperous orderly London (1.2). Looking at the streets of a working-class town, he decides: 'it was like war, but without the spirit of defiance war usually raised' (3.1). The bombing of London is the background to *The Ministry of Fear*. Reading 'let not man prevail' in a missal, the hero reflects that in the world at war man has prevailed: 'it wasn't only evil men who did these things' (1.6.2). War is the natural condition of man, according to these novels.

Most of us, however mindful of the appalling and dizzying state of things, do not normally live on that assumption. If we did, we should not read thrillers: the appeal of Leithen's running like a thief through the streets of London depends on a breach of the normal. During the blitz, sales of Anthony Trollope are said to have soared; Greene read *Barchester Towers* while travelling on lawless roads in Mexico, where a thriller would have lost its point.[96] *The Ministry of Fear* draws on memories of nights as an air-raid warden, but it was written in the relative peace of West Africa where Greene was sometimes reduced to hunting cockroaches for excitement. Perhaps the natural condition of man is between war and peace: most people hanker for thrills when they feel secure, and for security when violence makes life more exciting. Greene is interested in the 'edge' between these states and his thrillers look at relations between two kinds of normality.

Buchanite plots produce the same excitements in these novels as in *A Gun for Sale*. D. plays hide and seek with *them* – agents of the reactionary cause at home. He has a mission, to buy coal for the Republican (revolutionary) government and to succeed he must preserve his 'papers' which *they*, of course, are after. Outnumbered, the agent has to recruit an accomplice; the little hotel-maid Else hides the papers in her stockings. D.'s comment on the hiding-place reminds us of how much this sort of story is ruled by its conventions; 'the whole future of what was left of his country lay in the stockings of an underpaid child' (1.2). Greene can make his narrative compelling enough to keep us from smiling at the convention. When *they* murder Else and frame D., he finds himself trapped, in a very Buchanesque scene at his country's embassy, and escapes by a blow to a policeman's throat and a clutch at the gun, all related in the stream of short sentences which readers of thrillers accept when the writing moves easily and fast, although a fragment out of context falls flat.

> Forbes said, 'Drop that gun, you fool. This is London.'
> He took no notice of him at all. He said, 'My name is D.'
> (1.4)

The chase continues until on the last page D. sails away, with the girl his adventure has won him – although, since this is Greene, no more of a happy ending than that grudging concession to romance. D.'s point of view dominates; melodrama, for him, is normal life. If we read with a degree of scepticism about all the chases and narrow escapes, he frequently checks us with reminders that in his country war has made them natural. The thriller's mode, he urges in effect, is more real than our sheltered sense that life is not like that.

The heroine, Rose Cullen, who sails away with D. to revolution and civil war, is in a sense converted to the conventions of the book she belongs to. She ridicules them, in the early stages. D. travels with her from Dover, after his arrival, full of an agent's unease, and she tells him: 'I can't stand melodrama'. When they stop at a roadhouse where someone sends D. a note, he becomes even more melodramatic. She thinks he is playing 'the mystery man'. Why not send a note in reply?

> 'I wouldn't want to give him a specimen of my handwriting. He might forge it.'
> 'I give up,' she said. 'You win.' (1.1)

This is a common ploy to win the reader to the point of view of the spy, agent or adventurer, by stressing how wrong everyday life is going to be proved. The more convincingly its atmosphere is established, the more effective the air of adventure: and Greene uses the words of a popular song (as he uses the chorus girls' songs in *A Gun for Sale*) to persuade us that the agent has entered the world we know. 'You said "My heart is yours" – but you'd only lent it.' 'It's muck isn't it?' Rose comments, 'But it has a sort of appeal' (1.1). Inwardly, D. wonders how a country can spare time for such nonsense. This makes us more prepared to believe in him, and brings out the discrepancy between their points of view. When later he tells her that someone has shot at him in a London street, she protests.

> I don't believe it. I won't believe it. Don't you see that if things like that happened life would be quite different? One would have to begin over again.

She finds the bullet, and he explains Greene's doctrine that without commitment 'nothing matters at all' (2.1). England needs to learn, it appears, that bullets are to be expected in the street.

Bombs are exploding there in *The Ministry of Fear*. The English continue to hold jumbles, however, and the apparent innocence of a fête attracts Arthur Rowe. He wins a cake which contains a photograph of secret papers which *they* are soon active to recover. Greene began the novel, he says, with the idea of writing 'a funny and fantastic thriller' but found the story less funny as it developed.[97] Rowe has been convicted for the murder of his wife, whose illness he pitied, but released after the shortest detention because of the circumstances of the 'mercy-killing'. He feels guilty, knowing the deadly nature of pity. The adventures which follow his acquisition of the cake cause him to believe himself guilty of a murder he has not committed. When a bomb blast wipes out his memory of adult life, his convalescence in a mental hospital leads to further skulduggery. Events are fantastic, and at times amusing. Rowe consults a private detective agency when he fears that *they* mean to kill him. Mr Rennit has always dealt with adulteries and breaches of promise; he disapproves of murder investigations 'outside of story-books' since murderers are rarely gentlemen: 'This is a respectable business with a tradition. I'm not Sherlock Holmes' (1.2). The background of war adds piquancy to this distinction, and so does the villain Hilfe's observation that murder pays in the modern world: 'think of how many of your statesmen have shaken hands with Hitler' (1.3). Mr Rennit disapproves of war, too, because it 'plays hell' with his business – 'the reconciliations – you wouldn't believe human nature could be so contrary' (1.2). But he looks forward to a spate of profitable sexual irregularities when peace returns. Mr Rennit is a remarkable instance of a corrupt innocent – revived as Mr Parkis of *The End of the Affair* – on whose mind the bombardment of London makes no impression, and whose confidence in respectability tells him that violence does not signify outside story-books. Such invincible ignorance arouses Greene's sense of humour. So does the commuter at a London railway station during a bombing raid, who ignores Rowe's dramatic last confrontation with the armed Hilfe, while complaining bitterly that he has missed his train to Wimbledon. Such characters explain why Greene's novels tend to sympathise with criminals. Rowe, gently confessing to Mr Rennit that he is a murderer, is more a hero of our times than those impervious to the ministry of fear.

Greene tells us that *Our Man in Havana* (1958) originated in his experience of secret service naïveté when writing reports to London from his post in Freetown during the war. An earlier attempt at a comedy about espionage had been tentatively set in the Estonia of 1938. Visits to Batista's corrupt but agreeably louche Havana in the 1950s suggested an apter time and place for light comedy. The novel might have been darker, and more than an entertainment, if Greene had taken more seriously the conflict between Batista's ailing regime and Castro's revolutionary forces. But his adventures in Cuba in 1957 were 'as absurd a comedy of errors as anything . . . in *Our Man in Havana*' and its mood was relaxed. Defending himself against a possible charge of lack of commitment – to Castro's cause – he says, fairly, that he dealt only with British ineptitude, for which Havana happens to be the background.[98]

The secret-service British are committed innocents. Hawthorne, our man in the region, tells the Chief, 'I think we've got the Caribbean sewn up now, sir' [in the first of the 'Interludes']. The Chief explains that to run an agent one must understand him, and proceeds to picture our recently recruited man in Havana as a hero of 'the Kipling age' – pleasing to his idea of how the Caribbean should be kept safe from non-British interference. Hawthorne has in fact recruited Wormold, a gentle innocent who sells vacuum cleaners and worries about his teenage daughter Milly. The story of how he finances Milly's extravagances (horses, Country Club) and invests for her future by drawing expenses for the 'agents' he invents, and later by drawing 'plans' of a secret weapon he pretends to have discovered copied from parts of a vacuum cleaner, is among the most delicately elaborated jokes in post-war fiction. The more fantastic his reports, the more delighted the Chief, who suffers a nightmare when told by an expert that one of Wormold's drawings looks like a giant vacuum cleaner: '"Fiendish isn't it?" the Chief said, "The ingenuity, the simplicity, the devilish imagination of the thing"' (2. Interlude). Such a weapon, capable of sucking up the whole British fleet, belongs to the stories in boys' comic papers whose idyllic absurdities Greene has in mind in passages like this.

Since the real world punishes adult innocence, our man's enterprise brings cruel results. Convinced that things have become 'too big' for him alone, the Chief sends out Beatrice, from his pool of secret girls, and a radio operator. *They* (whoever they are) are persuaded by this show of British strength that Wormold must be taken seriously. They find real equivalents to the imaginary characters in his list of agents, rather as a critic treats a *roman-à-clef*; a young man he has decided to 'kill' in game is killed in earnest. Wormold's friend Dr Hasselbacher, involved with *them*, has his life's work wrecked before he is killed by a caddish agent called Carter. An attempt is made to kill Wormold, who later shoots Carter. Greene's flair for balancing comic and sinister effects creates a blend of farce and thriller. This novel's sceptical, likeable policeman, Captain Segura, hopes to marry Milly and keeps a suspicious but friendly eye on her father, comparing him to a child who innocently activates poltergeists. Their game of draughts played with whisky miniatures, each bottle to be drunk when captured, nicely causes the Captain's will to win to defeat him; for when the winner passes out, Wormold borrows his gun to settle with Carter.

The story ends as happily as can be expected; the Service hushes things up, buying Wormold's silence with an OBE and a job in England, training agents. He also wins Beatrice, who makes a speech about the folly of patriotism, and delights in his having fooled the foolish patriots. Yet the novel is true to its epigraph, 'But the sad man is cock of all his jests' – a line, surprisingly, from George Herbert. Dr Hasselbacher was growing a culture in his lab with the dream of a great discovery, which was his cause for living; when *they* destroy it, he ages suddenly, and Greene's summary of what has happened to him is a kind of reproach to levity: 'A whole mood of life had suffered violence' (2.3). The novel has other moments of which that seems true. Wormold's grief about Dr Hasselbacher is sharper because he has effectively betrayed his friend. 'If only we had been born clowns', he reflects, 'nothing bad would happen to us except a few bruises and a smear of whitewash' (1.3.3). The thought arises while he is brooding about God. He is a sad unbeliever; Milly has been brought up as a breezy convent-school Catholic; religious questions are well below the surface in this book. But it entertainingly reminds us what clowning causes in an evil world.

Wormold's loyalty is to love – of his daughter not his country –

and Greene's only claim on behalf of his later novel about the British Secret Service, *The Human Factor* (1978), is that it succeeds as a love story.[99] Castle loves his black South African wife, Sarah, and he considers himself 'a naturalised black' whose wife is his country. He gives secrets from his Southern African subsection of 'the firm' to the Russians, repaying a debt to the Communist Carson who smuggled Sarah out of the Republic when Castle's activities there on the firm's behalf had endangered her. Their successful marriage, in a small house in Berkhamsted, is something unusual in Greene. He found it easier to present suburban happiness sympathetically, perhaps, because it is not complacent but threatened, by Castle's treason. It is doomed indeed by the plot, which sends him to Moscow in the end and leaves Sarah, with her young son Sam, trapped in England. Loyal, anxious and dignified, Sarah is one of Greene's (too few) successful and appealing female characters. Castle's sense of the beginning of the estrangement from Sam as the child, starting prep school, becomes conscious of his blackness, is also very effective.

The scene in which he reads to Sam from Stevenson's *A Child's Garden of Verses* is the centre of many ironies. He begins with 'Keepsake Mill'. '"There are verses in childhood", he thought, "which shape one's life more than any of the scriptures"' (4.2.4).

> Over the borders, a sin without pardon,
> Breaking the branches and crawling below,
> Out through the breach in the wall of the garden,
> Down by the banks of the river, we go.

'What are borders?' Sam asks, and 'What's a sin without pardon?' 'Are they spies?' The idea of spies always excites him, so that the word often teases Castle at home, where he drowns, in J. & B., his fear of discovery. It is 'a sin without pardon', in his mother's opinion, when she learns that her son is in Moscow, having crossed his last border. He crossed his first when he married Sarah. The most dangerous border he crosses later this evening. This is after Sam has asked for his favourite poem from *A Child's Garden*, 'Windy Nights'. The poem tells of a mysterious galloper who, Sam says, is not white 'like you and Mr Muller' but black – and 'all the white people are afraid of him'. Castle knows that he cannot protect the boy from the resentment these words express. Mr Muller is a big man in the South African agency BOSS, who has been to the house in connection with the 'Uncle Remus' plan, for a 'Final Solution' to the black problem, should the need arise. Castle has Muller's notes and now he makes a copy of them, to hand on. 'He was', as Sarah had once put it, 'going too far.' That phrase has other ramifications. He has gone further than he has known in helping the Russians only with African materials and has been used in a way which readers of Greene's disciple, Le Carré, will find familiar. His superiors have gone too far in 'eliminating' his colleague Davis, an implausible part (which Greene says he regrets) of an otherwise realistic thriller.[100] It succeeds in its aim of persuading us to value Castle's kind of commitment, arising from love, over the patriotic allegiances demanded by East and West; and in entertaining, sometimes by flirting with self-parody:

> 'Well, I'm not sure about God, but you can certainly thank the K.G.B. (One mustn't be dogmatic – they may be on the same side of course.)' (6.1.3)

But *The Human Factor* never achieves the dramatic force of the closing scenes of *The Honorary Consul* which Greene wrote when he had temporarily abandoned the other book; Castle's escape from England is exciting but only at the level of a very good thriller.

Some of the entertainments are, like fables, stories constructed from a single idea. *The Tenth Man*, a novella written in 1944, and like the short thriller *The Third Man* (1949), intended for cinema adaption, was lost in the depths of MGM and forgotten about until its discovery and publication in 1985. Three out of thirty French prisoners, during the German Occupation, are to be shot. They draw lots and the rich lawyer Charvel takes a marked paper. When he seeks to buy a blank, offering all his property, including a country estate, impoverished and sickly Janvier agrees to take his place for the sake of his mother and sister. After the war, Charvel takes a job, incognito, in his old home where the sister lives in hatred of the man who has enriched her. Other ironies develop when a false Charvel announces himself. The proposed film was never made. It would pose a challenge to a director, especially in the atmosphere and timing of the drawing of lots in prison, and in the tone of sardonic comedy in which the tragic story is told. For actors there would be brilliant possibilities – in the role of Janvier, for example, transformed into a proud and commanding man of property for his last night in the cell. In reading, the shock of realising that a lifetime of poverty could give wealth an attraction stronger than the fear of death just prevents Janvier's being funny.

Loser Takes All is an amiable story about love and money. Set in a grand hotel in Monte Carlo, it demonstrates the appeal and the danger of a casino. Its hero Bertram almost loses his newly married wife Cary and his 'integrity' when he discovers a gambling 'system' which has 'the devil' in it and therefore succeeds. Winning a fortune, he forfeits Cary to a poor student, Philippe, and wins her back when he renounces the money, leaving Philippe ensnared in the 'system' at the casino. Money's allure is lightly and wittily acknowledged, so that the glaringly obvious almost looks new: 'one adapts oneself to money much more easily than to poverty: Rousseau might have written that man is born rich and is everywhere impoverished' (2.1). Greene takes advantage of the way rich people are vulgarised by grand hotels, to vent his hatred of them; enslavement to money looks especially nasty in the capitalist gambler known as A. N. Other, or 'the Other' – Greene's term elsewhere for the devil. The association of gambling and capitalism, satirised in this character, is more attractive in the story's other rich man, Dreuther, who argues against trying to 'domesticate adventure'. Everyone, he urges, is ambitious, but most people disguise the fact, gambling cautiously with their lives. His own ambition is without limit, and he is a winner. The story shows how Dreuther's wealth makes him powerful and dangerous to poorer people, but it gives him the charm of generosity and worldliness. He is based, Greene tells us, on a friend, Alexander Korda.[101] Cary counters his cynicism by arguing the cause of modest means (not quite of poverty) and she is, very attractively, allowed to be a harmless innocent, although her kindness to Philippe does him no good. Reunited, Bertram and Cary decide to gamble for fun, in future, without a system which might be too successful.

This story might have been one of the ambiguously moral and immoral tales told by Aunt Augusta in *Travels With My Aunt* (1979), which is Greene's pantomime – 'the only book I have written for the fun of it'.[102] She announces its tone in her opening words, 'I was present once at a premature cremation' (1.1). Following picaresque convention, she expands the book by telling anecdotes which merge merriment with macabre and indecent overtones, part of the fun lying in the respectable reactions of her nephew, the primary narrator. Her stories assist in his belated education. Henry Pulling has always lived carefully in the safety of suburban England. Unmarried and all but friendless, he cultivates dahlias – and a more quizzical, Greenean outlook on life than we might expect of a retired provincial bank manager. An ancient but still vital adventuress, his aunt, who (as we guess long before Henry learns) is really his mother, takes him on her travels and gives him a taste for pleasures which involve a little risk.

The setting is, for once at least, Greeneland. Their first trip is to Brighton, the next, by train from Paris, to Istanbul where a policeman reminiscent of Hartep in *Stamboul Train* awaits them. Aunt Augusta's lover, a minor war criminal, is called Visconti after the Viper of Milan in Marjorie Bowen's story which Greene says first made him want to be a novelist.[103] One of the liveliest characters met on the travels is a delightfully innocent American girl on her way to Vientiane. Henry's last journey is to Paraguay, via Corrientes which was to be the setting for *The Honorary Consul*. The aunt's lifelong milieu has been the demi-monde of 'tarts' – as defined by Jones in *The Comedians*. He and Brown belong to it, and Brown's mother Madame la Comtesse, who has never checked whether her title exists, must have encountered Augusta in some grand hotel – which they doubtless left with their bills unpaid. Bad cheques, undeserved public-school ties and euphemisms characterise it; Henry is very slow to grasp what his aunt means by her time 'on the stage'. This is Greeneland to those who know it best in Greene. Henry is educated into a whimsical version of Greene's idea of the real world, where crime and evil are not necessarily the same, where Catholicism does not mean accepting all that Catholics believe, where boredom and smug respectability are next to Godlessness. The tour of settings of earlier books is not nostalgic and Greene is as up-to-date as ever. Wordsworth, Augusta's black lover, substitutes pot for Henry's (official) mother's ashes, to foil the Detective-Sergeant John Sparrow (who is unaware that he shares his name with the Warden of All Souls). Sparrow tracks the drugs to Henry's dining-room and appeals to his good sense: ' – you wouldn't want to see that urn every day and wonder, are those really the ashes of the dear departed or are they an illegal supply of marijuana?' Graver matters are lightly treated, sometimes in self-parody; Augusta has her fortune told: 'There's a cross. Perhaps you find religion. Or it could be a doublecross' (1.5). But the prospect of death shadows the fun and at the close Henry, turned smuggler, has learned that a life which is *mouvementé* (in the *mot juste* of Visconti whose patron was Goebbels) is at least preferable to a dull old age where death stands 'as close as the bedroom wall.' (2.4) The last words of all, Browning's

> God's in his heaven —
> All's right with the world!

are in ironic relation to the novel's clowning, very far from, say, Wodehousian optimism.

6

A Region of the Mind

Greene is proud of his allegiances. It can seem that his credo is
the opposite of E. M. Forster's 'I do not believe in Belief'.[104]
But he believes, rather, in questioning belief from inside, and in
knowing the worst about humanity before choosing an allegiance.
Joseph Conrad's *Heart Of Darkness*, which shows how far
Europeans have forgotten or deceived themselves about the
'abomination' which lies beneath the surface of civilisation, is a
story to keep in mind when reading Greene. He is not polemical
in the sense of being a Catholic novelist or a novelist of the
Left. His novels are not intended to persuade us to become
Catholics or Socialists, but to show why their author believes
that the most drastic actions of Catholics and Communists are
preferable – in Doctor Magiot's words at the end of *The
Comedians* – to the indifference of an established society. The
innocents who ought to know better, the successful and the
complacent, the uninvolved comedians of his books, may be
believers – Pyle dies for democracy and Rycker thinks himself a
good Catholic – but because they are blind to the real world,
which appals and dizzies the characters who see it honestly,
their allegiances are worthless. Even so, the novels imply that
any committed action is better than apathy. Greene is passionate
in his support for victims and in his hostility, not so much to
those who victimise, since he holds evil to be natural, but to
those who take no notice. In this respect readers abroad tend to
find him exceptional among modern British novelists, and it is
one explanation of his enormous foreign readership.

His basic allegiance to any victim is the essence of the
humanism which he sees as common ground for Catholics and
Communists – very far removed, though, from any optimistic
trust in human nature. English readers who see that as a

strength in his work to which even suburban liberals may respond do not usually require a novelist to have the 'intellectual position' which readers in France, Italy or Argentina expect of any writer claiming to be more than an entertainer. Greene attracts attention abroad, and from academic exegetes in England and America, because he creates the impression that his novels conceal a formula which, if discovered, will explain everything. Such a key to all Greene's mythologies, connecting his eccentric Catholicism and his ambiguous attitude to Communism, may be sought by those who want it in a very broad background indeed. Pascal, Jansenism and theories of Grace; existentialism and the New Theology or existentialism and Jean Paul Sartre; Teilhard de Chardin and evolution towards the Omega point; Péguy, Unamuno and the role of doubt in belief – these are a few suggestions. Readers who wish to interpret Greene as a Catholic or as a political novelist have ample scope for exploring his 'labyrinthine ways'.[105] There are warnings in the novels against the pursuit of any one theory. Father Jean in *A Burnt-Out Case*, who used to be a distinguished moral theologian, now poses as a film fan, and is ashamed of his past. One reason why Greene is a novelist and not a theologian or philosopher is that he can be interested by such various, sometimes incompatible theories; he is as quick to see what a character in a novel might make of a new idea from his reading as to sense the fictional possibilities of a new place found in his travels. The view that God's nature is evolving suits the disordered mind of Father Rivas in *The Honorary Consul* as well as the ramshackle *barrio* where he makes his last Quixotic stand for justice. There is another warning; there are signs in published interviews with Greene of an urge, common among creative writers in England, to tease critics who would confine them in theory.[106] Suspicion among the Nobel jurors that he is less than systematic may explain why he has not won the Prize for Literature.

He would certainly resent, none the less, any attempt to associate him with 'the English Ideology' which distrusts theory, especially foreign theory, and favours compromise, decency, liberalism, detachment, obliquity, agnosticism in religion (although Catholicism and Anglo-Catholicism can be seen as acceptably eccentric) and moderation in politics (although to have been a Communist in the 1930s is regarded as a fashionable phase of growing up).[107] Evelyn Waugh, Anthony Powell and Henry Green are the other novelists of Greene's generation (all were at Oxford when he was) most highly valued by these criteria, which have been those of many English critics and reviewers. Waugh, Powell and Green share a sense of social superiority which finds very different expression in their novels but makes a detached, amused outlook more natural to them than it is to Greene, who shares their social and cultural background but not their willingness to write from inside it. They would not have written with his tone of satisfaction that 'an old dog-toothed civilisation is breaking now' (1940).[108] Powell might later have given the words to his ludicrous left-wing intellectual, Quiggin, in *A Dance to the Music of Time*. Whatever the shortcomings of civilisations, Powell would say, worse follows when they break. Behind his work and Henry Green's there is a stoical, aristocratic acceptance of given conditions and an intelligent enjoyment of their absurdities. Waugh despaired of the modern world and turned to fundamentalist Catholicism and an impossibly romantic conservatism. Greene sympathised with his despair. He says of Waugh's early comic novels that they are 'pure fun' and notes that when his satire became serious in *A Handful of Dust* (1934) the fun disappeared.[109] Waugh's *Scoop* (1938), however, is pure fun. Waugh, Powell and Green would not have agreed with Greene that a late 1930s setting was 'too dark for comedy' or that another setting, in the 1950s, seemed 'allowably comic' since its target (in *Our Man in Havana*) was the Cold War.[110] The '*allowably* comic' is a conception which distinguishes Greene from his ablest contemporaries, and from many younger British novelists of the last thirty years.[111]

He differs from most of them in his immediate appeal to readers outside the English-speaking world. Kingsley Amis's novel *I Like It Here* (1958) contains a tribute to Greene as an expert in the sphere of 'abroad' which alarms its typical Amis hero, Garnet Bowen.

The new Graham Greene, like most of the older Graham Greenes, was about abroad. Extraordinary how the region kept coming up. There must be something in it: not all the people who thought so were horrible.[112]

Bowen lectures to foreign students who put awkward questions about 'your Grim Grin'. What they would make of Amis is hard to imagine. Bowen's 'horrible' expresses a peculiarly English dislike of pretentiousness. A foreign student can identify Greene's horrible people easily: Amis's buffoons from *Lucky Jim* on reveal their egotism in bogus tones of voice and affectations difficult to interpret without close knowledge of the region of middle-class England to which they belong. Much post-war English fiction is social satire intended for English readers. We can imagine Pyle as a Fulbright scholar in Powell or Amis, Rycker as a pseudo-academic in David Lodge, or the Smiths as eccentric idealists in Michael Frayn; but in those fictional worlds they would be satirised by the criteria of English social comedy, amusing in their deviations from English norms of behaviour or good sense. Greene has just as good an ear for nuances of speech and manners, but his characters represent types of modern folly which readers in most parts of the world can identify. He writes for the foreign students as well as for Kingsley Amis.

Two recent works have reasserted his allegiances and the conspicuous concern with big issues which, perhaps, best explains why his appeal is so very widespread. *Doctor Fischer of Geneva or The Bomb Party* (1980), a novella, is a study of evil and *Monsignor Quixote* (1982), a short novel, portrays a good man. Each achieves what the novelist can do better than the philosopher or the moral theologian, creating the atmosphere, tone and feeling which make a style in the largest literary sense – 'a region of the mind'. The characters belong to Greene's now fifty-year-old fictional world, and yet have an air of the 1980s. The writing is spare, and conveys all Greene's unmistakable tones of voice from light mockery to sardonic scorn, with an effect of effortless ease. The stories are composed as if to disprove the theory that narrative is 'inauthentic' today; they offer a very personal, intensely conceived rendering of values which are vaguely dispersed in contemporary society. They are most distinctly Graham Greene's in their ambiguity about comedy, which is inadmissable or horrible in *Doctor Fischer*, natural but close to pathos in *Monsignor Quixote*.

Doctor Fischer is Greene's quintessential villain. He is a toothpaste millionaire, so rich that the richest people in Switzerland fawn upon him. Although he has reached the limits of worldly success, he still believes in it, and jeers at his son-in-law, Jones, who lives modestly by translating business letters. He is said to have 'a smile of infinite indifference' (15); some of his circle of 'Toads' as his daughter Anna-Luise calls the rich toadies are truly indifferent people, without souls, but Fischer has suffered at least a mean jealousy of his wife – now dead – who found a friend to share her love of music (hated by Fischer). He has used his money to avenge himself, in a Switzerland where his degree of wealth apparently assures almost unlimited power, and esteem. Estranged from his daughter, his only remaining interest is in his power. He thinks of himself in theological terms. Believing that God is hungry for our humiliation, he plays God accordingly: the rich guests at his parties endure humiliations – cold porridge while he has caviare – in exchange for costly presents. When Jones points out at the end that if he so despises the rich he must despise himself most of all, he agrees and commits suicide. Since Fischer talks of hating God and trying to hurt his Son, we can read the story as a Christian fable about theological despair leading to damnation but this reading is suggested, not imposed. Jones, as narrator, despairs when Anna-Luise, a delightful innocent, dies in a skiing accident. The sight of the doctor's corpse destroys his 'small half-belief' in God. Whether or not we can accept the idea of damnation, Doctor Fischer is a fine picture of what it might look like, especially in the party scenes, which are the best in the book. Kingsley Amis complained about a party in an earlier novel that it is 'designed to show what a terrible thing it is when people set about enjoying themselves'.[113] Greene's distaste for conventional conviviality reaches an extreme expression in Fischer's parties where the simpering toadies are obliged to laugh at the doctor's gruesome jokes at their expense. 'We have much fun' one of them explains to Jones. At the bomb-party the guests pick out of a bran-tub packets which contain very big cheques, despite a warning that one packet contains the bomb. The comedy is blacker because Fischer's urbane conversation keeps plummeting to an infantile level of humour.

> 'Prizes for what?' I asked.
> 'Certainly not for intelligence', Doctor Fischer said, 'or the Divisionnaire would never win anything.' (9)

If not inadmissible, comedy in his company is infernally unfunny.

Monsignor Quixote is a good innocent because he is an unsuccessful, unambitious priest, who lives humbly with the knowledge that he is somewhat ridiculous. Whereas Doctor Fischer is absolutely certain in his hatred of God and contempt for humanity, Quixote is doubtful and preaches the Greenean creed that a living faith must be shadowed by doubt. He lavishes affection, absurdly, on his old car 'Rocinante' and, unsuitably, befriends a Communist Mayor whom he calls Sancho. He is out of favour with authority when the story begins, because his bishop disapproves of his low birth, scanty learning, and absurd claim to be descended from a fictional character. When chance makes him a monsignor, he and Sancho, drinking vast amounts of wine, take to the roads of Spain in Rocinante. Their innocence causes trouble everywhere, and they are pursued by the authorities – the Guardia Civil (windmills who 'revolve with every wind'), and the bishop, who has Quixote brought home, and threatens to have him put away after he has uttered the dreadful words 'Bugger the bishop' (2.1.1). While all Switzerland admires Doctor Fischer, almost all of Spain is against the gentle, foolish, Christian monsignor. He takes refuge, when the Guardia gun down Rocinante, in a Trappist monastery; and here he dies, at the altar, performing with his fading mind a strange, defiant Mass, although under 'suspension' and without wine or Host, for the benefit of the atheist Sancho. At the end of *Doctor Fischer* Jones puts the question: 'Evil was as dead as a dog and why should goodness have more immortality than evil?' Sancho wonders why Quixote has left him feeling a love which outlives death.

This is an escapade, on a finely calculated small scale, in 'the tragic-comic region of La Mancha'. Some contemporary novelists would have made much of the difference between Quixote's world and the reader's, emphasising the fictionality of fiction. Greene's characters accept the hero's descent as a pleasant fiction. A wise Trappist monk says that the difficult distinction between fact and fiction is too complicated for words. Greene's whimsy has the lightness of touch essential if a book is to be more than whimsical.[114] Greene chose La Mancha for the region of his fiction because the quixotic is supremely paradoxical and doubtful. Don Quixote is a clown and a hero, deluded and yet right in his commitments, determined to live in a better world than really exists. *Monsignor Quixote* begins as pure fun and moves to a climax which is too disturbing to be quite solemn, and too moving to be absurd. Greene's Quixote often feels ashamed of his sense of humour because 'a solitary laugh is so often a laugh of superiority', the opposite of 'the laughter of joy' (1.9). He enjoys the joke of his 'ancestry'; his half-belief in his ancestor is his only vanity. The Mayor tells a Marxist parable about a Prodigal Son revolted by his father's bourgeois prosperity but 'unable to situate himself in the class struggle' because *Das Kapital* has not yet been written; luckily an old peasant explains capitalism to him while they are carrying swill to the pigs. The monsignor comments that this revised version sounds as boring as his breviary, and adds, 'I am glad you left in the pigs' (1.4.1). He feels remorse when, absent-mindedly, he demonstrates the Trinity with two bottles and one half-bottle of wine he and Sancho have had with their dinner. It is anathema to imply that the Holy Ghost, represented by the half-bottle, is inferior to the Father or the Son – 'it was condemned expressly at I forget which Council' (1.3). They correct the heresy by drinking another full bottle, and next morning Quixote is able to smile at his mistake. He is usually ashamed of laughing, as he is when the Mayor finds him unsuitable lodgings: 'It's very wrong of me to laugh. But I just thought: what would the bishop say if he knew? A monsignor in a brothel' (1.7). He hopes God will forgive him for laughing at the Mayor's satirical remarks about Father Heribert Jone's *Moral Theology* – a forbidding German work. It is recommended to him by a humourless young priest:

'Oh of course, one accepts the Gospels naturally,' Father Herrera said in the tone of one who surrenders a small and unimportant point to an adversary. 'All the same, Jone on moral theology is very sound.' (1.2.2)

Quixote is too modest to laugh even at that.

Sancho is inclined to laugh without scruple. He sees that a priest is a kind of Quixote and calls the monsignor's favourite devotional works – St John of the Cross, St Teresa, St Francis de Sales – his books of chivalry, irrelevant nowadays. He thinks himself a man of the modern world, believing in *Das Kapital*, and in pleasure; he has been in prison (more comfortable than a monastery, he says), but knows the best brothels and restaurants. As he comes to like and respect Quixote, all Greene's allegiances come together in the principles they share. Each has a cause, but each can doubt it and feel that friendship comes before loyalty to State or Party or Church. Monsignor Quixote's death recalls many of the most impressive scenes in earlier books, including the last days of the whisky-priest and León Rivas. Quixote has fought a small battle and been injured by a censer, trying to halt a corrupt religious procession. When he sleepwalks to the monastery chapel and gives the non-existent Host to Sancho, we are uncertain whether he is dying a madman, or performing a small miracle. But he dies asserting faith and friendship, defying reality – including the authority of the Church – and we feel that he has triumphed over his realistic, authoritative, humourless bishop in the comic spirit of his ancestor, which Greene thinks is the right spirit for a priest, or for any believer.

Notes

1. Robert Browning, 'Bishop Blougram's Apology', lines 399–404. Quoted in *A Sort of Life* (Penguin edn, 1974), p. 85.
2. *Ways of Escape* (Penguin edn, 1982), p. 58.
3. Ibid., p. 167.
4. Walter Allen, in *Contemporary Novelists*, ed. James Vinson and D. L. Kirkpatrick (Macmillan, 1982), p. 276.
5. See 'the Virtue of Disloyalty' in *The Portable Graham Greene*, ed. Philip Stratford (Penguin edn, 1977), pp. 606–10.
6. See also *Ways of Escape*, p. 207. Many passages of this book first appeared in the Introductions to the Collected Edition.
7. *A Sort of Life*, p. 58.
8. *Ways of Escape*, p. 67.
9. *A Sort of Life*, pp. 11, 21.
10. *Collected Essays* (Penguin edn, 1970), p. 83.
11. Ibid., p. 108.
12. *A Sort of Life*, pp. 54–5.
13. Ibid., p. 54n.
14. Ibid., p. 57.
15. *Collected Essays*, pp. 319–20.
16. Ibid., p. 13.
17. Ibid., p. 169.
18. Ibid., p. 343.
19. Ibid., p. 345.
20. Philip Stratford, 'Unlocking the Potting Shed', *Kenyon Review*, 24 (Winter 1962), 129–43, questions this story and other 'confessions'. Julian Symons, 'The Strength of Uncertainty', *TLS*, 8 October 1982, p. 1089, is also sceptical.
21. *A Sort of Life*, p. 80.
22. Ibid., p. 140.
23. Ibid., p. 145.
24. Ibid., p. 144.
25. Ibid., p. 156.
26. W. H. Auden, 'In Memory of W. B. Yeats', 1940, line 72.
27. *The Lawless Roads* (Penguin edn, 1971), p. 37
28. Ibid., p. 40.
29. *Ways of Escape*, p. 175.

30. Ibid., p. 195.

31. *A Sort of Life*, p. 157.

32. See 'François Mauriac', *Collected Essays*, p. 95; and *The Quiet American* (3.1.1) where Fowler and Vigot discuss Pascal.

33. See *Ways of Escape* pp. 193–4.

34. Ibid., p. 197; and *A Sort of Life*, p. 121.

35. Ibid., 197–8. See also *Monsignor Quixote* (1.6) where the monsignor and Sancho talk about Unamuno.

36. *Ways of Escape*, p. 145.

37. A. Calder-Marshall, 'The Works of Graham Greene', *Horizon* (May 1940), 367–75.

38. Francis Hope, 'True to Formula', *The Observer*, 16 September 1973, p. 36.

39. *Ways of Escape*, p. 226.

40. Ibid., p. 74.

41. Ibid., p. 28.

42. See Stratford (ed.), 'The Virtue of Disloyalty'.

43. Calder-Marshall, 'The Works of Graham Greene', pp. 368–9.

44. *Ways of Escape*, p. 220.

45. Ibid., p. 198.

46. See *Ways of Escape*, pp. 22–5. Twentieth Century Fox made a film version, very badly according to Greene, 'though not so bad as a later television production by the BBC'.

47. William Tufnell Le Queux (1864–1927) was a very popular author of cloak and dagger novels, and according to his own account, a spy.

48. *Ways of Escape*, p. 182.

49. *Great Soviet Encyclopaedia* (Collier Macmillan, 1975), vol. 7, p. 406.

50. Bernard Bergonzi, *Reading the Thirties: Texts and Contexts* (Macmillan, 1979), pp. 68–89, discusses frontiers in literature of the period.

51. Admitting that the novel was in general poorly received, Greene notes the praise of V. S. Pritchett, Ezra Pound and Ford Madox Ford. *Ways of Escape*, p. 28.

52. See *Ways of Escape*, pp. 26–9.

53. Ibid., pp. 16–18.

54. G. Wilson Knight, *The Wheel of Fire* (Methuen, 1949).

55. C. S. Lewis, *The Screwtape Letters*, 1940 (Fontana edn, 1982).

56. *Collected Essays*, pp. 98–9.

57. See Frank Kermode, 'Mr Greene's Eggs and Crosses', *Encounter*, 16 (1961).

58. M. Merchant, *Comedy* (Methuen, 1972), p. 67.

59. See 'Beatrix Potter', *Collected Essays*, pp. 173–80.

60. *Ways of Escape*, p. 31.

61. Ibid., pp. 30–1.

62. Miguel de Unamuno, *The Tragic Sense of Life* (Fontana, 1962), pp. 311–12.

63. *Ways of Escape*, p. 31.

64. Cyril Connolly, *Enemies of Promise* (Penguin edn, 1961), p. 82.

65. See Bernard Bergonzi, *Reading the Thirties*, pp. 60–5, for a discussion of Auden and Greene.

66. *Collected Essays*, p. 98.
67. Cf. *The Heart of the Matter* (2.1.2) where Father Rank's laugh sounds like the bell of 'a leper proclaiming his misery'.
68. Quoted in *Geoffrey Madan's Notebooks*, ed. J. A. Gere and John Sparrow (Oxford University Press, 1981), p. 75.
69. 'Rider Haggard's Secret', *Collected Essays*, p. 159–60.
70. *A Sort of Life*, p. 39.
71. *Collected Essays*, p. 86.
72. Cardinal Newman, *Apologia pro Vita Sua* (1864), Chapter V.
73. *A Sort of Life*, p. 145. The lines are from *Kidnapped*, Chapter 10.
74. *Ways of Escape*, p. 64.
75. Evelyn Waugh, 'Felix Culpa?', *Tablet*, 5 June 1948, and *Commonweal*, 16 July 1948.
76. 'The End of the Affair' by Ian Gregor; from Ian Gregor and Brian Nicholas, *The Moral and the Story* (Faber, 1962), pp. 192–206.
77. *Ways of Escape*, pp. 93–4.
78. Ibid., p. 94.
79. Greene says that 'perhaps Scobie should have been a subject for cruel comedy'. *Ways of Escape*, p. 94.
80. Ibid., p. 108.
81. *Ways of Escape*, p. 198.
82. Ibid., pp. 60, 198.
83. Ibid., pp. 120–42.
84. Some of Greene's Catholic admirers had used this idea from the sixteenth-century Spanish saint's *En una noche oscura* (In a Dark Night).
85. The novel's dedication to Docteur Michel Lechat, who had worked at the Congo *léproserie* at Yonda when Greene stayed there, pays a tribute to the Fathers of his mission.
86. See *Ways of Escape*, pp. 203–7.
87. Ibid., p. 25.
88. See above, pp. 18–19.
89. *Collected Essays*, p. 160.
90. *Ways of Escape*, pp. 26–7.
91. P. N. Furbank, reviewing *Travels With My Aunt*, *The Times*, 22 November 1969, p. v.
92. *Ways of Escape*, pp. 68–9.
93. *Collected Essays*, p. 167.
94. *Ways of Escape*, p. 54.
95. *Collected Essays*, p. 334.
96. *The Lawless Roads*, pp. 33–4.
97. *Ways of Escape*, p. 74.
98. Ibid., pp. 183–5.
99. Ibid., pp. 228–30.
100. Ibid., p. 229.
101. Ibid., p. 167.
102. Ibid. p. 220.
103. *Collected Essays*, p. 16.
104. The opening sentence of his essay 'What I Believe', 1939.
105. *The Labyrinthine Ways* was the American first edition of *The Power and*

the Glory, a 'difficult and misleading title', according to Greene, *Ways of Escape*, p. 67.

106. See Philip Stratford, 'Unlocking the Potting Shed'.

107. See Bernard Bergonzi, *The Situation of the Novel* (Macmillan, 1976, 1979), for a discussion of 'the English Ideology'.

108. In 'At Home', *Collected Essays*, p. 336.

109. *Ways of Escape*, p. 199.

110. Ibid., pp. 184–5.

111. William Golding is a notable exception.

112. Kingsley Amis, *I Like It Here* (Victor Gollancz, 1984), p. 22.

113. Kingsley Amis, 'Slow Boat to Haiti', *The Observer*, 20 January 1966, p. 27.

114. It resembles only superficially Giovanni Guareschi's Don Camillo stories.

Select Bibliography

The place of publication, unless stated, is London.

GRAHAM GREENE

The Collected Edition (Heinemann/The Bodley Head) includes Greene's Introductions. The Viking Press, New York, publish the Uniform Edition. Penguin Books, Harmondsworth, publish paperbacks. *The Name of Action* and *Rumour at Nightfall* have not been reissued.

Novels and novellas

Published by Heinemann:

The Man Within (1929)
The Name of Action (1930)
Rumour at Nightfall (1931)
Stamboul Train (1932)
It's a Battlefield (1934)
England Made Me (1935)
A Gun for Sale (1936)
Brighton Rock (1938)
The Confidential Agent (1939)
The Power and the Glory (1940)
The Ministry of Fear (1943)
The Heart of the Matter (1948)
The Third Man and *The Fallen Idol* (1950)
The End of the Affair (1951)
The Quiet American (1955)
Loser Takes All (1955)
Our Man in Havana (1958)
A Burnt-Out Case (1961)

Published by The Bodley Head:

The Comedians (1966)
Travels With My Aunt (1969)

The Honorary Consul (1973)
The Human Factor (1978)
Dr Fischer of Geneva or The Bomb Party (1980)
Monsignor Quixote (1982)
The Tenth Man (composed 1944) (The Bodley Head and Anthony Blond, 1985). Includes two film sketches

Short Stories

Nineteen Stories (Heinemann, 1947, was reissued, enlarged, as *Twenty-One Stories*, Heinemann, 1954). The Bodley Head issued *A Sense of Reality* (1963); *May We Borrow Your Husband?* (1967); and *Collected Stories* (1972)

Plays

Three Plays (Heinemann, Mercury, 1961), contains *The Living Room* (1953), *The Potting Shed* (1958) and *The Complaisant Lover* (1959). The Bodley Head has published *Carving A Statue* (1964) and *The Return of A. J. Raffles* (1975)

Autobiography and travel

Journey Without Maps (Heinemann, 1936)
The Lawless Roads (Heinemann, 1939)
In Search of a Character: Two African Journals (The Bodley Head, 1961)
A Sort of Life (The Bodley Head, 1971)
Ways of Escape (The Bodley Head, 1980)
Getting to Know the General (The Bodley Head, 1985)

Essays

The Lost Childhood (Eyre and Spottiswoode, 1951)
Collected Essays (The Bodley Head, 1969)
The Pleasure Dome, ed. John Russell Taylor (Secker and Warburg, 1972). Collected film reviews
Greene has also published: *Babbling April* (Basil Blackwell, 1925) – undergraduate poems; *British Dramatists* (Collins, 1942); *Why Do I Write?* (Percival Marshall, 1948); *Lord Rochester's Monkey* (The Bodley Head, 1974) – a biography composed in the 1930s; *J'Accuse – The Dark Side of Nice* (The Bodley Head, 1982); *The Little Fire Engine* (Max Parrish, 1950), and three other 'Little' children's books with the same publisher.

CRITICISM

Allott, Kenneth and Farris, Miriam. *The Art of Graham Greene* (Hamish Hamilton, 1951)
Atkins, John, *Graham Greene* (Calder and Boyars, 1957, revised 1966)
Bergonzi, Bernard, *Reading the Thirties: Texts and Contexts* (Macmillan, 1978)
Calder-Marshall, Arthur, 'The Works of Graham Greene', *Horizon* (May 1940)